The Co-op Revolution

To Art & Laura,

Co-operatively Yours!

Jan DuGlass

July 11, 2019

Copyright © 2019 Jan DeGrass

01 02 03 04 05 23 22 21 20 19

All rights reserved. No part of this publication may be reproduced, stored in a retrieval system or transmitted, in any form or by any means, without prior permission of the publisher or, in the case of photocopying or other reprographic copying, a licence from Access Copyright, the Canadian Copyright Licensing Agency, www.accesscopyright.ca, 1-800-893-5777, info@accesscopyright.ca.

Caitlin Press Inc.
8100 Alderwood Road,
Halfmoon Bay, BC V0N 1Y1
www.caitlin-press.com

Text and cover design by Vici Johnstone
Copy edited by Christine Savage
Printed in Canada

Caitlin Press Inc. acknowledges financial support from the Government of Canada and the Canada Council for the Arts, and the Province of British Columbia through the British Columbia Arts Council and the Book Publisher's Tax Credit.

Library and Archives Canada Cataloguing in Publication

DeGrass, Jan, 1950-, author
     The co-op revolution : Vancouver's search for food alternatives / by Jan DeGrass.

Includes index.
ISBN 978-1-987915-95-2 (softcover)

     1. Food cooperatives--British Columbia--Vancouver. 2. Food supply—British Columbia—Vancouver. 3. Food industry and trade—British Columbia—Vancouver. 4. Food—Social aspects—British Columbia—Vancouver. I. Title.

HD3450.V36D44 2019   334'.50971133   C2018-905966-4

The Co-op Revolution

Vancouver's Search
for Food Alternatives

Jan DeGrass

Caitlin Press

CONTENTS

Foreword/Forward — Rick Scott	6
Intro — What the Thousand Words Could Not Say	9
Making a Food Revolution	11
Life is Just a Bowl of Canaries	20
My Ontario Roots	31
"Money, Money, Money"	40
Going for Broke	50
Beekeepers and Storekeepers	58
Ms. Cheese and Honey	63
With a Little Help From My Friends	76
Travels and Teardowns	90
Food, Glorious Food	96
Give Us Bread but Give Us Roses	102
A Change is Gonna Come	115
Blowing in the Wind	122
Tito's Yugoslavia	132
What Happened Then?	141
Going Faster, Like a Roller Coaster	148
And Today?	156
Photos	162
Appendix I — Alex Berland	173
Appendix II — Fed Up Co-ops Operating in BC—1976	179
Bibliography	183
Index	185
Acknowledgements	190
About the Author	192

foreword/forward

by Rick Scott

I'm introducing this book with a bit of a chuckle, because I find myself writing a foreword about looking back. In songwriting, this kind of phrase is fodder for a verse.

I am now age seventy, and for me to reflect on the 1970s is to take the measure of a lifetime. I came to Canada in 1970. The summer day I arrived in Vancouver, the Deluxe Brothers were having a full-on water fight with the Out to Lunch Bunch in the middle of Fourth Avenue in Kitsilano. Water pistols, hoses and bucket brigades—hilarity was stopping traffic, and I knew this was my kind of community.

Community was birthing a lot of things at that time—a genesis of ideas seeking a lifestyle centred on peace, love, alternative energy, gender equality, organic veggies and safety for all. Utopia it wasn't.

The part I played, quite literally, was as a musician in the fledgling BC folk scene, which gave me a unique window on the times. I toured far and wide with Pied Pumkin and Pied Pear, performing at countless concerts, dances, and BC folk and children's festivals, and also at fundraisers for the recycling group SPEC and for Greenpeace, raising roofs and saving whales.

We and many other musicians provided the unique soundtrack for a renaissance that was busting out all over: socially, politically, spiritually and artistically. And to me, all these were intertwined and of almost biblical proportions. Cue the trumpets and begin the begats! For instance: The Pleasure Faire begat the Easter Be-In and Renaissance Fairs, which begat the Habitat Festival, which begat the Vancouver Folk and Children's Festivals, then rock festivals, jazz festivals, accordion festivals and a thriving music industry.

A similar genesis took place in the co-operative movement. Have you ever been amazed at how a tiny sunflower seed produces a towering majestic bloom containing thousands more seeds? So it is with co-operatives.

By the 1980s, when my family moved into Community Alternatives (CAS) co-operative housing at Second and Maple, there existed co-op businesses, banks, restaurants, food sources and transportation. CAS designed and built its own apartment building, a farmhouse in Abbotsford with an organic salad business, and Muffin Works bakery on Commercial, which hired folks with disabilities. It was also a partner in Isadora's restaurant on Granville Island. CAS went to great lengths to be inclusive of all ages, ideas and abilities. My oldest son and my daughter-in-law worked at the Uprising Breads Bakery and Horizon Distributors food warehouse.

In a co-op, everyone does everything. I was not good at meetings and as a musician didn't know what I could offer. So the CAS community proclaimed me "vibe watcher," and I sat in the corner with my trombone until language got dangerous or emotions ran too high, at which point I would stop the proceedings with eight bars of intentionally inane blat. Gig of a lifetime with lyrics by *Robert's Rules of Order*.

For some time I was a member of the vacuum cleaner committee. Our task was to find the best and most practical device for our building. The process was long, slow and often seemingly absurd, but it worked! And I learned the art and value of consensus, which has served me well throughout my life and career: slow going on the surface, but always in steady motion.

Being a touring musician in the 1970s was a spartan existence, travelling by van in which we often also slept, dining and bathing by the kindness of others. One luxury was the ever-present, lovingly preserved jars of Tunnel Canary peaches, cherries and pears. They seemed pricey but well worth it; an army moves on its stomach. At the time I had no idea they came from the CRS Workers' Co-op; they were simply manna from heaven.

Decades later I'm still making music and am the curator of a tiny museum on a tiny island. My love of history is rooted in my love of story and an ever-growing understanding of how important it is to remember and document the past.

If you display a frying pan, no one cares or notices, but if that's the skillet that Grandma Tooley attacked the bear with to save the school children…well, folks will stare at it in amazement.

And so it is with this story of a small tribe of people working to make their dreams and beliefs a practical reality. Times have changed, dreams have evolved, but it's increasingly important to remember an era gone by, that sourced so much of what we take for granted in our lives today. Get comfy, crack open a jar of your favourite preserves and enjoy this taste of history.

—Rick Scott, Protection Island, www.rickscott.ca

Introduction

WHAT THE THOUSAND WORDS COULD NOT SAY

In 1999 I was invited to submit an entry on the topic of co-operatives for the *Encyclopedia of BC*, an ambitious project to usher in the new millennium. It was a difficult task. In just one thousand words I had to encompass the entire history and development of the organizations and summarize the roles of BC's food and housing co-ops, and its producer and worker co-ops.

Although I had been involved with pretty much every co-op in Vancouver during the 1970s, there was one in particular that had generated the most passion in me. I had been a founding member of CRS Workers' Co-op, an organization that operated a cannery (Tunnel Canary), a food wholesaler (Brokerage Collective, later called Horizon Distributors), a beekeeping operation (Queenright) and a bakery (Uprising Breads).

The work was difficult, yet it was a job I loved. My parents, my former teachers and my landlord could not understand my zeal for what seemed to be boring food wholesaling and retail sales employment. I couldn't understand why they were satisfied with their lives. Education, entertainment and stimulating conversation were always on hand with my lively co-workers. We were performing socially useful work. We were not misguided hippies—we were on the right path. It was the rest of the world that was screwed up.

I was reminded of these times spent in co-operative endeavour when I stopped by Uprising Breads Bakery many years later, sometime around 2002. One of the salespeople, a youthful, energetic woman, was wearing a black T-shirt with silver lettering. The words marked an anniversary of CRS, which she told me had been celebrated at a picnic not too long ago. Certainly it had been a T-shirtable event and she was clearly proud of the occasion, though hazy on the details.

"Was it a bakery anniversary or a CRS anniversary?" I asked.

"I'm not sure," she replied. Although I had been a founder, I had not been invited, and I was mildly miffed. No, I was *really* miffed. Did she know that she wouldn't have a job that day if I hadn't helped build the co-op?

"When was the anniversary exactly?" I asked.

"Summer," she said.

"That's not what I remember," I said.

That's when I knew I had to write this book.

Chapter I

MAKING A FOOD REVOLUTION

When I joined my workers' co-op in 1975, I had arrived fresh from Ontario, where I had lived in a communal house while studying Russian literature at the University of Waterloo—a dead-end career path, as I had belatedly come to realize. Our five household members were vegetarians, and we bought our food through our own small co-op. "Food for people, not for profit," we chanted as we loaded bulk bags of granola and healthy broccoli into our backpacks. News filtered from across the country about some heavyweight co-operators in BC who had started a chain of co-ops like ours; it was with awe that we learned they had set up a central warehouse in Vancouver—all owned and managed by people like us.

I had to go and see.

Besides, travelling to Vancouver had become a ritual pilgrimage for our age group. It was reported that you could busk on the street for money or pot, that there was a beach where you could go nude and that you could live in the woods, brush your teeth in a creek and breathe in the pure air. "But don't try to hitchhike there," I was warned by those who had gone before. Most of them had become stuck by the side of the road in Wawa or Thunder Bay, forcing them to call their parents for bus money. I would avoid that problem by taking the train and getting a job when I arrived. I would be independent—an anti-establishment, twenty-something, active woman.

But after arriving in Vancouver and enduring a discouraging round of interviews at employment centres, I decided to contact an organization known by the acronym of CRS that was operating under a government make-work grant. (At that time the initials stood for Consumer Resource Services, but it would later become Collective Resource and Services Workers' Co-operative.) I hoped there was a chance of working in an area that I enjoyed: food co-ops. Ros Breckner answered the phone from what I later learned was a home/office on Pandora Street, and she invited me to view their latest project, a fruit cannery that was in the process of being set up in North Vancouver. She spoke with an air of efficiency; there was no sign of the laid-back attitude I had come to expect from the West Coast counterculture. They had farming friends in the Okanagan, she told me, who were shocked by the amount of good food wasted after harvest simply because it couldn't get to market. This cannery would help small farmers by purchasing the fruit and preserving it for resale. CRS was operating a worker-owned industry! These people were truly starting a food revolution.

By this time I was living in a mansion on Angus Drive in Shaughnessy, the wealthiest part of the city. I had rented one of two small rooms in an attic that had once been servants' quarters, while my landlady, Mrs. Stone, lived below me in the palatial home. She explained that after the sudden death of her husband, who had taken charge of the household finances, she had no idea whether she had the funds to keep up the aging house, so she had immediately sought lodgers. She seemed glad of the company and was kind enough to provide towels and bedding for me, this young woman who had arrived with only her pack on her back. Entrance to my room was up the back stairs, and I had a great view of the North Shore Mountains. The other bedroom was occupied by a handsome Quebecois mine worker who admitted he had never lived in anything but a clapboard house prior to this. We shared a tiny kitchen that had been carved out of a closet and was entered by walking through the bathroom. (Fortunately, the toilet had its own closet.) Though batts of fibreglass insulation hung between the beams of the unfinished space and I had to wash my few thrift store dishes in the bathtub, the antiquated casement window let in the morning sun. The rent was inexpensive, but I was aware that to others it would appear that I lived in luxury.

Ros offered to pick me up for my first visit to the cannery; she explained that some of the CRS project workers often carpooled, so this was not an imposition. I was ready and waiting nervously when her ugly, functional Austin drove up the magnificent circle driveway of the mansion and past the sprawling rose bushes. I later learned that her other passenger, Floyd Norman, had said to her, "You're going to take *this* car up *that* driveway! Are we allowed?"

With Ros at the wheel, we drove across the Lions Gate Bridge into North Vancouver, the sprawling suburban community that sits in the rain shadow of mountains on the north side of Burrard Inlet. She drove down a major hill on Lonsdale Street toward the water then suddenly turned into an alley just below First Street and pulled up in front of one of a row of gloomy buildings painted in dull browns and greys. The cannery at #2, 216 East Esplanade had no windows on its alley side, and its major features were a loading dock and a giant garbage container that took up half the parking lot. The air stank of pickled herring and industrial solvent. Seeing my wrinkling nose, Ros pointed to the fish cannery, Fjord Seafoods, next door. We entered a gloomy hallway that opened into a white, bright, high-ceilinged space littered with a jumble of metal fittings. People began arriving at once; I was hastily introduced to a teenage couple, arms linked, who told me they were volunteers helping with the cannery project. They moved to the high open windows on the far side and continued to cuddle, gazing out over the esplanade's view and murmuring to one another. Floyd, who had ginger-blond hair, a beard and a gold ring in one ear, reminded me of a Viking. He towered over the couple as he immediately began hefting pieces of equipment and fitting together the jumble of metal parts with deft, confident movements while Ros ran to answer the office telephone. When a courier arrived with a large parcel marked Fragile, Ros appeared momentarily to collect it, muttered something to me about jar samples and returned to the office.

Floyd beckoned me over to show me the boiler that was the cherished object of everyone's attention—they were in the process of repairing this aging giant so that it could provide steam pressure for the cannery. Having no knowledge of what a functioning boiler should look like, I could only nod wisely and keep my silence.

A plumber entered carrying two giant toolboxes; he plunked them down with a frown and looked around. "Chaos as usual," he said aloud. Turning to me, he asked, "How'd they rope you in?" This skeptic's name was Al Poole, and I offered to help him get started by cleaning his tools. "You're not helping the cannery, you know. You're just helping me," he said.

"I'm not quite sure what to do—it's all new to me," I replied.

"Just imagine the cannery finished and do whatever needs to be done," he advised.

Since everyone was occupied with tasks, I decided to check out an office tucked away near the entrance that had room for two small desks and a half-size fridge with a hotplate atop. The desks brimmed with serious-looking forms, plates of congealed food, scrap paper, a teapot and an ancient adding machine. I started to tidy it.

That first day at the cannery was a blur of images and information delivered by this diverse crew of workers, a confusing orientation that undermined my self-confidence, but nevertheless, I knew I wanted to learn more. I wanted to be a part of it. There was no hiring committee, no form to fill in, no request for a resumé; it appeared that if I hung around long enough, asking questions and hauling equipment around the cannery floor, I was hired. You had to be a self-starter with this organization.

In the first few weeks of set-up, the cannery collective consisted of Ros, who was one of the founders of the organization; Floyd, who also worked with another of the CRS projects, the beekeeping collective; Jean Hogan from Salt Spring Island; and the addition of another newcomer, a tall, lean, clean-shaven fellow, Roger Inman, who had arrived from Winnipeg carrying his tent on his back and had somehow found out about the cannery. Though he had no previous experience at co-operatives or canneries, Roger was greatly enthusiastic.

As it turned out, my friend Al, the plumber, was not one of the collective, but he had been hired to complete all the necessary steam fitting during the set-up. This philosophical wielder of the pipe wrench wanted one day to write about his trade, and after a brief flirtation he shared with me a sample first line from his book: "Plumbing is a bitch." At first he grumbled a lot—it was work outside of his usual scope of blocked drains and hot water pipe assembly. It was especially disturbing to him that so many of the willing helpers setting up the cannery were volunteers, idealistic co-operative people who asked him endless questions. But as the weeks wore on and the cannery took shape, he loosened up and eventually became a loyal supporter of the co-op's work.

The set-up of a cannery required much attention to detail. The equipment—canning retorts, steam canning baths, cooling tanks, steam-jacketed kettles and stainless-steel counters—came from the Ball Corporation, and I was handed a worn copy of the home canner's bible, the *Ball Blue Book*, a compendium of recipes and useful tips, which I read from cover to cover. Because our recipes would be made on a larger scale than a home kitchen, the measures had to be calculated by someone who knew their arithmetic—thankfully not by me. I was the newbie who was rapidly learning all the steps that a business start-up entailed. It was a refreshing world away from the pages of Dostoevsky and Tolstoy.

"I need to know more," I told Ros one day, and on my own initiative I took a recreational evening course in home canning at a local school and was horrified to learn how much sugar it took to produce a jar of grape jelly. Buying a can of Welch's grape juice and adding sugar and pectin was not my idea of a quality product. Our jam would be different, we decided—less sugar, more fruit—and it would appeal to customers, we hoped, even if we had not yet found our market niche. We would study up on the many qualities of healthy honey that we planned to use in preserving the fruit, and would learn how to adapt it for our recipes.

It was also a time to get to know the CRS members who worked at the other industries under the same umbrella: Queenright, the beekeeping collective that fabricated wooden bee boxes and kept hives; the Brokerage Collective, a food wholesaler that was in the early stages of planning; and the storefront food co-op organizers who were assisting volunteers in starting their own co-ops throughout BC.

One of the storefront organizers, Dana Weber, had first become involved in co-ops while living in Victoria, and both he and Ros were fond of reciting, at the drop of a hat, the origins of the so-called "new wave" of food co-ops. It had begun, they told me, in Victoria in 1971 with a pre-order, prepay co-op called Amor de Cosmos (named after

BC's second premier, whose adopted name meant love of the universe), and it was run by its members. This group of like-minded people had banded together to order in case lots from wholesalers for a better selection of good, wholesome food at cheaper prices. When they picked up their orders, all members would participate in dividing up the cases, pails or sacks in a church hall or other volunteered space. This idea caught on, and soon Amor's weekly order totalled in the thousands of dollars because groups as far away as the Gulf Islands were ordering through the Victoria co-op—only later realizing that they could set up their own.

By 1972 twelve co-ops in BC that were run by the people they serviced saw the need for a central warehouse in Vancouver, a co-op of co-ops that could be a distribution point for the smaller ones, a place where goods could be received from suppliers and packaged for sale to the smaller co-ops. This developed into the Fed Up Co-operative, which would be an instrumental force in the province's new-wave co-op movement, as it became a central hub in Vancouver for co-op information imparted mostly through its newsletter, called *The Catalist.*

The name Fed Up had a double meaning. "Mom, I'm all fed up," might be said after eating a big meal, and it was also a play on words that mocked another old-guard mover in wholesale goods, Federated Co-operatives, the organization with the distinctive red CO-OP logo.

The first Fed Up warehouse was situated in an old church at Franklin and Commercial Streets. By 1976 it had moved to a warehouse at 304 East First Avenue, close to Main Street, where it would remain for many years. Fed Up had a vital role and a commitment to an ideal that became the genesis of the workers' co-op.

Along with Ros and Dana, Gail Cryer was another early member of CRS, one of the organizers hired to plunge into the development of the storefront co-ops. These retail spaces were deemed more suitable for urban centres than the pre-order, prepay model, because customers in the city were used to shopping daily and they were comfortable pushing a cart around a shop to select their goods.

The East End Storefront Co-op on Vancouver's Victoria Drive opened its doors in 1975, the same year I arrived in Vancouver, and it looked much like any other small grocery store—with the difference

CRS Workers' Co-op member Gail Cryer gave a helping hand to the set-up of various storefront co-operatives.

that it was run by its members, who bought shares in it, took turns working in the store and had a say in what items were carried. All the CRS members shopped there, of course—so I did too. For many months I never saw the inside of a large chain supermarket, which was no loss as far as my peer group was concerned. The East End Co-op was small and neighbourly. Safeway was big and impersonal. Small was beautiful; big was bad.

Ros and Dana's involvement in Fed Up had been propelled along the way by a man who was a legend in the co-op movement, Paul Phillips, who I never came to know very well. At the time that I met him in 1975, he dressed in thrift store bargains and usually wore a leather headband that had become his trademark. He was a flamboyant personality

A young Sylvia Kenny tests the Tunnel Canary apricots.

with a huge Welsh-accented voice that filled any room or public arena. Gail Cryer remembers watching him galvanize a crowd during an organizing meeting, jumping in at just the right moment to incite the audience to action—in this case, to form a co-op. With her background in community organizing, she realized that he was someone to learn from.

Ros had met Paul when she moved to Victoria, fresh from a relationship breakup. A friend who shopped at the newly formed Amor de Cosmos Co-op took her there for her first food distribution. Paul and Dana, who were living in Victoria at the time, came in the door to collect their order, and Ros noticed Paul right away. "He was always full of himself," she recalls, "and I thought, *I never want to get to know that person.*" Of course, later they became the best of friends.

The eccentric, quick-witted Paul was of the ilk that Ros describes as BMOs, Big Male Organizers. BMOs are the ideas people, the guys who start things; they come up with great ideas and find people to put the ideas into action. "But if they stay on in an organization," Ros points out, "it doesn't work. You need other types of people to sustain it." BMOs are distracted by more and better ideas that they want to ignite in others. It is the people they inspire who do the real work of sustaining the project.

Paul Phillips did not work in the cannery, though he had a huge hand in deciding its future, and he recruited other interested workers who moved to Vancouver to be a part of the burgeoning co-op movement. Born in England and raised in Wales, Paul had immigrated to Toronto in 1958. He was arrested for sedition at a Vietnam War protest rally in America, and when he was kicked out of the country, he came to Victoria, where he helped found the Amor de Cosmos food co-op at the St. John the Divine Church, which served as the distribution centre. He applied for and received a federal grant to expand food co-ops, and he worked in Vancouver to grow Fed Up's food distribution network until it extended as far as the Queen Charlotte Islands, with weekly trade exceeding eighty thousand dollars. After Fed Up, Paul returned to Victoria to work with House Savers, a group developed by Spring Ridge Housing Co-op to break apart condemned houses and salvage their building materials. It was not until after his death in 2012 that I learned that among his other careers, he had once been a touring banjo player and performed with Pete Seeger and Phil Ochs.

It was Paul who had initiated the cannery after reading about a compact canning operation that could be set up in a trailer to go to fruit-growing centres in the US, thus allowing local people to can on site. He proposed a similar travelling trailer to go to BC's Okanagan, because at that time, the early 1970s, the tree fruit marketing boards kept a tight grip on trafficking in fruit—individuals couldn't transport their fruit for sale. However, the idea of CRS starting up a travelling cannery never came to pass. It was impractical and, as Ros remembers, none of the individuals involved wanted to move to the Okanagan. Then, with the change in the marketing board regulation in 1975 that allowed better access to fruit, the group of Dana, Ros and Paul quickly decided to set up the cannery in North Vancouver. To source the fruit, they turned to their friends Lee and Bob McFadyen, who farmed in the fruit-growing area of Cawston, BC.

Chapter 2

LIFE IS JUST A BOWL OF CANARIES

The Tunnel Canary cannery received its unusual name because Floyd, in an attempt to draw a prototype label for our jars, misspelled the word cannery. The Tunnel part of the name came from the fact that the building was located on a back lane a few blocks east of Lonsdale, and we were told that a railway tunnel ran underneath us. Our customers ascribed profound and unintended significance to the name: the tunnel canary was a bird that miners took with them down the shafts. When the air went sour and the bird died, it was an early warning signal to get out. Much later we learned, to our amusement, that a Vancouver punk rock band had used the name for their group.

A tunnel runs through it: we at the cannery were told that a railway tunnel ran beneath our building in North Vancouver and this landmark, plus a misspelling of cannery, gave rise to the name Tunnel Canary.

The space that was leased for the cannery had been used previously for food processing, and it had a walk-in cooler that met with health standards. To everyone's relief our refurbished boiler, which had to be inspected by an official, was also approved. Al's valves and pipe threading were done correctly. Ros and Roger, who had worked with him on the refit, were proud of the fact that this was accomplished by the end of May 1975, allowing us to start canning in June.

However, we were still scratching our heads over the operation of the equipment; it was a process of trial and error. When it came to selecting canning jars, we realized that the equipment we had installed from the Ball Corporation was designed for use with homestyle glass jars. The company that would sell them to us wanted us to take possession of over twelve thousand cases at once—a year's supply, at the cost of thirty-six thousand dollars. This was out of the question, even after we half-heartedly measured the basement of a collective member's home for storage space. Instead we chose commercial jars—at seven cents cheaper per jar than the homestyle jars and available in small amounts. They were standard, straight-sided 32-ounce jars with screw-on lids that came with a white resealable material inside their rims. With the application of heat, the jars would seal. We had no idea if this would work with our equipment, but thankfully it did.

During our trial runs we washed every new jar by hand, unnecessarily, until a sales rep from the container company demonstrated the sterility of the packaging. He was probably taking bets on the side as to how long we would stay in business. Even without washing the jars, the process was laborious.

Another big issue during set-up was dealing with the government. A federal government agency administered a three-year grant called LEAP (Local Employment Assistance Program), with the hope of creating jobs in new businesses. They required reams of reporting with forms to be filled in, giving an account of who was employed, what expenses had accumulated and what progress was expected. During our first month of operation, I was assigned the task of writing a progress report for the bureaucratic eye. Although I didn't keep a copy of that document, I recall its first words vividly, since I laboured over it for days. I recorded that the cannery had opened in time for "June's first blushing strawberries." In July the first of many government project officers stopped by to visit. Snickering, he inquired as to the author of the "blushing strawberries" report. My colleagues gave me up immediately, but all was well—it seemed I had enlivened the usual boring reports for the bean counters.

But the biggest issue was the development of a team, or a collective, as we called it. A woman who had been involved for many months in the cannery's set-up wanted to spend more time with her family. She tried to juggle the two jobs and was summarily cut from the group during an informal meeting, which I did not attend. The message was clear: We weren't playing. This was about business, about commitment. Each member had to show a time commitment or it wouldn't work.

Soon after, a job hunter was referred to the cannery by the Canada Employment Centre. He smoked a pipe, had an annoying drawl and explained honestly that he needed the salary in order to pay his gambling debts. He worked with us for three months before the axe came down on him, too. This time I attended the firing meeting and tried to soften the blow by suggesting other employment that would be more suitable for him. He was an avid reader, I had noticed, with an interest in current events. Several years later I met him in a downtown bookstore, where he had become the manager. Far from holding a grudge, he thanked me sincerely for my suggestion (though I didn't remember giving it) that he would be more suited to the book trade.

Finally the cannery collective was in business. The fruit came from the Okanagan. Ros and some of the others would rent a big Budget five-ton truck, drive to Cawston, camp overnight on Lee and Bob's land and return with fruit. "I was terrified to drive a five-ton," she recalls. "One time we burnt the brakes coming home." But the adventure was fun—it was after their return with the goods that the hard work began.

Wearing hairnets and aprons, we washed and packed the fruit in glass and stirred giant, steam-jacketed vats of jam with wooden paddles. The resulting products were delicious but labour intensive—it was hot, wearying work that had to be completed while the fruit was ripe, not before or after. Peaches had to be blanched in a hot-water bath to remove

The cannery cooler was filled with the fragrance of fruit—cherries, peaches, apricots, apples and pears—as each season unfolded. Strawberries, raspberries and blueberries were turned into jam sweetened with honey.

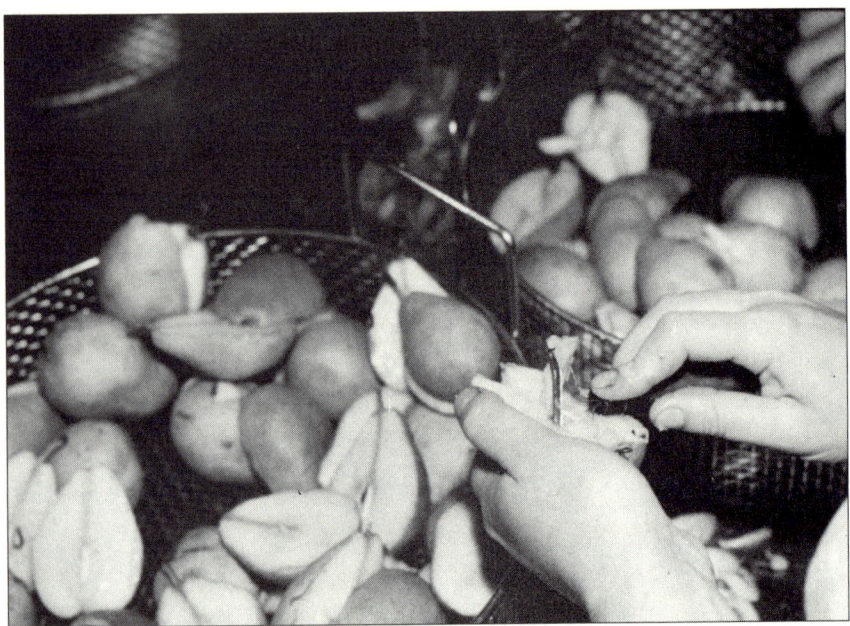
Pears had to be sliced, cored, peeled and packed in water to make their own juice.

their skins. A stainless-steel blade mounted on the counter sliced them neatly in half and also tore the pit from the fruit. Plums and tomatoes were easiest; cherries left our fingers scarred and purple. Finally we decided to leave the pits in the whole cherries, rationalizing that this would provide a more natural product and acknowledging that it was truly a pain to gut each cherry by hand. After sending a case of our cherries to one of our markets, a daycare centre, we received an anxious phone call from the supervisor. The preschool children were trying to swallow the cherries whole. The case would have to be returned for a refund.

Nonetheless, the cherries were a big hit, canned in either water or honey, as were the tomatoes packed in their own juice, and the apricots, halved or whole. Perhaps it was an accident the first time that we left one whole apricot kernel in a jar of fruit during processing, but we discovered that the flavour of the apricots was greatly improved by this almond-shaped pit, so it became a regular practice. Then one day when Paul Phillips phoned from Victoria to find out how the cannery was doing, Ros and I double-teamed on the phone line to talk with him. Ros explained how we had found that leaving one pit in every jar improved flavour.

(Left to right) Jan DeGrass, a volunteer, Ros Breckner and Roger Inman hard at work processing pears at Tunnel Canary cannery.

"Of course," he said excitedly. "It's from the prussic acid!" I was horrified, because I knew that another name for prussic acid was cyanide. After doing some research, we discovered that the kernels inside apricot pits contain amygdalin, which can potentially convert to cyanide. It was unlikely that one pit would poison anyone, and in fact, an extract of apricot pits called laetrile was later touted as a cure for cancer. The important thing was that no one died from our apricots in honey syrup, and many remarked on how flavourful they were.

Especially for vegetarians, we developed delicious green-tomato mincemeat without the traditional suet, and we also pioneered something called TC Sauce, a type of brown ketchup, not unlike HP Sauce. Unfortunately, it didn't sell and we were forced to halt its production.

All of these items were canned in a process similar to the hot-water-bath method of home canning, except that steam was used: racks of jars were set in a container and a bell-shaped lid was fastened over top. The rack of hot jars was then lifted out and cooled in a cold-water bath.

The package of equipment from Ball had also included a pressure-canning retort. We experimented with canning baked beans and aspar-

It was a grand day when the boiler that powered the steam equipment at the cannery passed official inspection.

agus in this. Ros was nervous about allowing these particular goods to be sold, so we kept them for ourselves. Low-acid vegetables such as beans and asparagus needed to be processed properly under pressure to kill possible toxins such as botulin. We never mastered the retort—but I do recall eating my Tunnel Canary canned asparagus on toast at home for lunch.

The jam, or "mélange" as we called it, was also popular, possibly because of the lack of demon white sugar. Our jams did not contain the regulation 60 percent soluble solids (i.e., sugar or honey), as it seemed to

Just showing off: Jan DeGrass proudly demonstrates the final product of canned beans from the pressure canner. Beans and asparagus were low-acid vegetables that needed to be processed properly in a pressure canner. We were nervous about selling these in the marketplace; they went home with us for our own lunches.

us that jam should taste of the actual fruit within and not be a diabetic's nightmare. But this meant that it couldn't legally be labelled as jam. It had taken several weeks of pondering and collective input to come up with the name mélange and no one was really satisfied with it, but we couldn't sell the jam until we complied with labelling regulations. It was an example of how little the governors of the food industry's health and standards in 1975 understood about the power of the embryonic wholefoods market and its producers.

We employed simple sales techniques, visiting potential customers—the food co-ops, Fed Up, health food stores and community organizations such as daycare centres—to sell them on the product. The food co-ops would be supportive, we hoped, and would buy our goods because they contained no preservatives or additives and had been made by a co-op industry, sisters and brothers in the "food for people, not for profit" movement. At least that was the theory. In fact they took some convincing since our prices were higher than other commercial canned fruits and jams. But our vision for an equitable marketplace that was run by worker-controlled industries continued to propel us forward.

With the cannery in full production during the summer of 1975, all other events were lost to me in a cloud of steam, the fragrance of sweet fruit and the relentless ache of my feet.

Then on the morning of October 3, 1975, we nearly lost threefifths of the cannery collective. That morning I had travelled to work by bus from my attic room, and I waited restlessly outside the building for the others to arrive in their carpool by the route they took from Vancouver's east end. I knew they drove over the Second Narrows Bridge into North Vancouver and onto the Low Level Road, which ran alongside the train tracks and the port grain elevators. As I waited, a tremendous explosion tore through the air. Startled, I looked up at the sky, fully expecting a jumbo jet to come crashing down.

A few minutes later a car pulled up bearing Roger, Ros and Dick McGinnis, the co-op's accountant/bookkeeper. They emerged, excited and still shaking. Roger reported that seconds—literally seconds—after their car had passed close to the giant wheat-pool elevators, one had exploded. The debris had missed hitting their car by a narrow margin.

Once out of the danger zone, they had pulled over immediately, and Dick had stood on the hood, peering back along their route. When the accident was reported in the newspaper, it was attributed to a buildup of dust within the elevator. The trio realized how close to death they had been when they learned that one of the grain workers died in the explosion and four more died later in hospital from burns.

On another occasion Roger and I were working alone in the cannery, boiling a batch of jam. Laughing and chatting, we didn't notice at first that the jam was pouring out of the spigot at a faster rate than was comfortable. Feverishly we jumped into action, sliding the sterilized jars under the spigot, wiping them off and capping them. Panicked, we yelled at one another, sweat dripping from our brows, until Roger had a brainwave. He reached over and turned off the machine.

"We can turn it off," we reminded one another.

We were in charge.

We were hopeful about our bottom line, and early in the summer we were already pondering what to do during the slow winter months when fruit was not available. We came up with several ideas that looked good on paper, including pickles, a big seller. But secretly I believe that everyone was looking forward to taking a break during winter.

In December 1975 Tunnel Canary cannery drew up its statement of income, as required by our grant funders, for the eleven months ending November 30. Our gross sales had hit $4,846, but the overall picture after expenses was of a loss of $2,791. Our expenses, including the big item—salaries—amounted to $39,094, giving us a net loss of $41,885. However, our LEAP grant made up much of that loss and allowed us to continue to build the business.

One late afternoon during that summer of 1975, after a strenuous fourteen days of working without a break, I walked out of the cannery, exhausted, got on a bus and travelled across town to visit my friend Jenna, who I hoped would soothe me.

"You're just tired," she said. "Phone and tell them why you left."

When Ros answered the phone, I announced dramatically that I was through with canning.

"It would be too bad if you were to leave the project," she told me gently, "just because of the cannery. Paul could use some help with the Brokerage Collective. Could you do that?"

"What does he do?" I asked. "What's a brokerage?" I added, pouting slightly that my exit speech should be met with such practical problem solving. I had pictured myself flouncing out of the group, pride wounded, never to return, with no one caring about my departure.

"He's developing a food wholesaler that can help us grow," she replied. "It's really needed. He'll tell you all about it…if you stay."

Humbly I accepted the offer, with the caveat that I would still work part-time in the cannery to help it through the fruit season. Thus began another six years of involvement.

> In September 1976, the price of a case of, for example, twelve 32-ounce jars of water-packed cherries was $13.08, while plum jam in a case of twelve 16-ounce jars sold for $10.80. Ours were high-end products, more expensive than the average fruit in stores at that time, yet we were selling to a cost-conscious market. We wrote an article for the Fed Up newspaper that explained our dilemma:
>
>> "In order for the cannery to be self-sufficient and support the five workers that it will need, we need to sell about $70,000 worth of food a year. We don't know yet if BC's co-ops are capable of giving us this volume. We are asking for your support."
>
> We offered a refund, if empty jars were returned in their cases, of $1.20 for the larger, 60¢ for the smaller. We were ahead of our time in this effort to recycle, as during the 1970s most glass containers, such as wine bottles, were simply thrown away.

Chapter 3

MY ONTARIO ROOTS

While I was working at the cannery that summer of 1975, farmers would occasionally show up at the door with baskets of fruit—usually not first grade, but good for canning—having had their goods turned down by the supermarkets. One such farmer begged to use our cooler to store his plums; the effort of getting his goods to market with no resultant sale had embittered him. I lobbied for him to have access to the cooler and wanted the collective to buy the plums rather than waste them. He thanked me for my efforts and asked, "You're a farm girl, eh?"

No, I wasn't—I had always lived in cities, Toronto and Ottawa among them, and I had lost touch with the way food was grown. It was involvement in our food co-op in Kitchener–Waterloo, Ontario, that had helped me to understand and appreciate the dedication of farmers.

In 1973 my then husband, Rick DeGrass, and I were students at the University of Waterloo, and we had moved into a shared home on Gordon Street in Kitchener. I also performed secretarial duties for the Germanic and Slavic department by typing in English, German and Russian, and I was fond of boasting that I could type anything. Our roommates, Peggy, Kevin and Gloria, were already knowledgeable about communal living, and if you lived in a shared house, you were fair game to help with any projects that your housemates were working on. Inevitably Kevin asked me if I would type the Waterloo Food Co-op's newsletter. I agreed. That was the beginning.

Today, when I ask others who started their own co-op associations in the 1970s, I hear a similar story. Ros and Dana started by doing small chores for their own food co-ops in Victoria. It was their responsibility as members to volunteer some time, and they became committed. The tasks were sometimes boring: taking inventory, packaging herbal teas or filling bulk containers and cleaning up after spilled goods. But while the work may have been tedious, the socializing was fun. The volunteers met and worked with like-minded others; they became friends, plus they all took home good food and considered that their small effort for the movement was the right thing to do.

I have only two of our Waterloo Food Co-op newsletters, which I have saved through the years. As you would expect, there were recipes such as Yummy Cheese Pie and Lemon Sesame Squares (any unhealthy ingredients were substituted with healthier ones to be found at the co-op), and there were also gripes about the reliability of volunteers or the number of meetings that took place in a democratically run co-op. Besides this usual chatter, many of the articles showed that members gave intense thought to the nature of the organization, particularly its faults, and to how it could be improved. One member grumbled, "Our meetings are plagued by complainers and suggesters who have no intention of seeing the problems through to the end. A good idea is useless unless the person who thought it up is willing to make sure it happens." This reflected the tenor of the times: In the words of American activist Eldridge Cleaver, "You're either part of the solution or you're part of the problem." This advice is as true today as it was yesterday.

Norman Taylor, a Waterloo Food Co-op member, wrote a philosophical paper destined for the operations manual of the co-op. In it he decried the bureaucratic structures of most organizations as dehumanizing:

> The efforts of people to effect a valid choice of organizations in which they wish to be involved has resulted in the formation of alternative structures....One of the alternatives, not new but rarely used of late, is the co-operative....It is of paramount importance that all members be aware of, and have a voice in, the decisions and operations of the group. Hence there is no need for stifling, rigid hierarchies of command. A member may contribute to the group according to his/her specific abilities, but because a member can have a working knowledge of the whole, he/she is able to move from task to task as the need arises.

This thoughtful paper, written in 1974, precisely foreshadowed many of the principles that inspired CRS workers. It sounds Marxist—but we didn't view it that way. The Marxist–Leninists were a small but active group in Kitchener–Waterloo during the 1970s, but we considered their efforts to be doctrinaire and rigid. They were scary people who mouthed slogans and asked lengthy, convoluted questions of speakers at rallies. We were more free-floating and open to all new ideas—Marxist economics was simply one of those ideas.

In our communal home in Kitchener, the five of us held discussions about the food co-op and how it could function better: we were in favour of the "warehouse model," which was conceived, I believe, by Kevin. Simply put, rather than run the co-op as a traditional storefront grocery store, as it was first designed, we would switch to a warehouse for greater efficiency of space and to avoid the financial loss experienced by the store. This loss could have come from shrinkage, spillage, shoplifting or the rising cost of storefront rent. In our new model, food would be distributed through the co-op's existing groups, members who were banded together by geographic location or "cells," as we called them. Our house was part of J cell, along with others in our immediate neighbourhood. I suggested that the designation J could stand for Joy—we would be called Joy cell. Others in our cell decided that J stood for Jell-O. Jell-O won.

This warehouse model was up against models thought up by other members: the "liquor store" model, for one, was based on the Ontario practice at the time of having liquor store customers consult a catalogue of alcoholic products, fill out an order form on paper and hand it to a clerk. These models prompted others to devise various compromises on the initial theme. Many of the ideas were brilliant, and I hope that some of the members went on to careers as planners and consultants because their ideas were somewhat wasted on a small food co-op in a middle-sized town in Ontario. Yet these efforts were the signs of growth in the movement.

With all this analysis came the desire to reach out to other co-ops—to be part of a larger movement, and to learn what others were doing and how they overcame their difficulties. It was also true that we thought we had something really good going in Kitchener–Waterloo, and we wanted to brag a little. We decided to call a Conference of Southern Ontario Food Co-ops, and we met in October 1974 at the campus centre of the University of Waterloo. Rick coordinated the event, and twenty-five guests showed up, a startlingly diverse group that opened our eyes to the breadth of the movement.

The Cabbagetown Co-op in Toronto was close to our own model of selling in that they added no markup and used volunteer labour. Yet it was also different; there was a strong sentiment within their co-op toward community support for working-class families and the working poor. They timed the co-op's days of operation to tie in with the arrival of members' welfare or pension cheques.

On the other end of the scale, an attendee from the Oshawa Co-op told us that they were supported by the United Autoworkers Union and that they occupied a sixteen-thousand-square-foot warehouse with full-time paid staff. This delegate to our conference said he did not believe that co-ops should be welfare organizations, and he made a point of stating that they were afraid of being ripped off, given that they offered low markups. He left the conference early and in a subsequent letter sent a cheque to cover our expenses, though we had not asked for one. He also noted that the conference was not what he had expected and criticized it as being poorly organized. He may have been correct about the lack of organization, as we hadn't known what to expect ourselves. We were, in fact, demonstrating a sound co-op principle: co-operation among co-ops. However, no future resolutions had come out of that conference and we had to deem it a failure.

Another couple from a co-op in Etobicoke—he in suit and tie, she in skirt and heels—stayed on after the conference for the evening potluck dinner. While sitting on the floor of a communal house, holding their mismatched plates in their laps, they told us that the first thing they had noticed, to their dismay, upon arrival at the conference was that they were overdressed. We told them that their apparel didn't bother us as long as our work shirts and peasant blouses didn't bother them.

So we were all different—but we were all joined by a common goal, with so many ways to experience that goal. It was around this time that we heard of the burgeoning co-op movement in British Columbia. My marriage to Rick was heading inexorably toward a breakup in early 1975, and I decided to set out by myself to see what was happening in BC. After working with CRS Workers' Co-op that year, in September I wrote back to my former friends and colleagues, those who lived at Fairview House as well as others in our Kitchener–Waterloo circle.

September 3, 1975

Dear Keith, Jim, Jill, Gene, Margaret, Ralph, Stu, Aiya, Ruth, Linda, Dave, and all friends, lovers and sometime dinner companions (did I miss anyone?),

In short, I'm writing this to anyone who is interested in what I have to say, and I certainly have a lot to say these days. It concerns personal stuff and co-operative stuff, but mostly co-operative stuff, because that's what I seem to be involved in so deeply these days. (Wow, brief flashback—it puts me in mind of the day so many months/years ago in the kitchen at Gordon Street, where I first told Kevin, "Yes, I will type the newsletter for the co-op," and that's where it all began.) Here it's just the same way. I phoned Fed Up one day soon after I arrived here in May and casually asked what I could do…if there were any jobs available? I'm now working with CRS, an outgrowth of the Fed Up Co-op Wholesaler. I started work at the cannery, one of the projects that CRS began on a LEAP grant from the government (hmm…more about that later), and I'm now working with both the cannery and the brokerage. It's an incredibly complex network of interrelated producer, wholesaler and consumer co-ops throughout BC. Fed Up alone has fifty member-run co-ops who order from the warehouse and also put in weeks of work on a rotating basis.

The production co-ops like the cannery (fruits and vegetables in home canning jars) and Queenright Beekeepers Co-op are all worker-controlled industries and intend to be self-supporting in the near future. There are numerous other affiliated and non-affiliated worker-controlled production and service co-ops both near and far away from Vancouver who tend to keep in close communication with Fed Up in a way that I could scarcely have believed possible. The scope of the network boggles me.

Why such a positive network has emerged in BC and not in Ontario is a question that I continually consider. There is no insular growth here as there is in the east—one co-op does not spring up in a vacuum here, but rather becomes involved immediately in a province-wide distribution and communication network. I just returned from a Fed Up Council of Representatives meeting in the north woods (moose land and canoeing)—at Ootsa Lake, to be exact—where Fed Up's member co-ops were all duly represented. Also represented there were, of course, CRS and its various projects, storefronts, cannery, etc., plus some other non-affiliated groups: someone from Consumers Action Association, someone from a housing co-op in Victoria, members of the Seattle Workers' Brigade (another vast co-operative network in Yankeeland) and so forth.

It was both elating and disappointing in many ways—elating that it could happen in such a together way and accomplish so much business to the satisfaction of all, and disappointing in that it was hampered by even more bureaucratese than the average Waterloo Food Co-op general meeting. (Is there a motion on the floor? Could you please put that in writing? Reports first, discussion later…and a speakers list, oh dear!) Whatever happened to the old anarchists? What was group consensus all about, anyway? But eventually everything did get talked through and we broke for study groups to discuss various common themes that had recurred. What is a production co-op's relationship to Fed Up? Shouldn't it be one of mutual support? How do we generate money for the Paid Collective to work in the warehouse without adding to the cost of food? We discussed the political line of the co-operative movement in general and its direction. Storefront co-ops and what they're all about. (Most of the co-ops buying from Fed Up are on a pre-order, prepay basis.) Just lately, storefronts on a member-run basis, like the early days of Waterloo, have been springing up. (Interesting that it's the reverse to the way it happened in Waterloo.)

What's this all about anyway: Paid people? Meetings run by *Robert's Rules of Order*? A grant from the government? My God—the Brokerage Collective (which consists of Paul and myself) is even working on importing coffee by the shipload, from a non-exploitative source, of course. A lot of energy for a nutritionally valueless drug.

There were many mental hurdles to my acceptance of some of the practices here. I receive a salary for my work with CRS and that salary is provided by a government grant. But I don't call it free money, and I believe that we are effectively guarding against our being co-opted by this money. We receive $700 a month, which works out to about $600 after deductions. We keep as much of that money as we need to live on, usually about $300 or less, and we kick back the rest of the salary into the project. No capital was provided for within the grant, and any specific project, like the cannery, pays for equipment and costs by using previous kickbacks from previous projects plus existing kickbacks from the workers. We generate capital from the grant funding in this way.

At the Fed Up warehouse, the Paid Collective (a recent innovation, by the way), who are not operating from a grant, generate their wages by finding cheaper suppliers for their goods. If they find a cheaper supplier, they calculate the difference between the older expensive item and the newer cheaper item and they take 50 percent of the difference and put it in a fund to be administered by the collective for paying their wages and warehouse costs, etc. The other 50 percent is passed on to the co-ops in the form of lower prices. I would be very interested in hearing what everyone thinks of this, either individually or collectively. Actually, everyone here would be interested in hearing what others think about it.

I am somewhat dismayed by the vertical (north/south) co-operation that has taken place on this coast. Fed Up has links with co-ops far up north and also with the Seattle Workers' Brigade to the south, which in turn has links with co-operative warehouses in Oregon and San Francisco—very vertical and very American. These mountains are a real barrier, it seems. I try to talk up horizontal co-operation with Ontario, but I am a still small voice.

To try and simplify things a little, all I really wanted to ask of you is in the local vernacular: "What's happenin'?" Is there still a co-op? Is there still a newsletter? If so, could someone send it to me? Is it all survival or is something really growing again? Is the cell structure still going strong? Oh, and this whole letter actually grew out of a simple discussion between Paul and myself over a supplier for safflower oil. Where did we get our oil from? (Remember those oil drums with blue printing on them?) Is it possible to give me a list of sources and suppliers for things: oil, grains, anything. In turn, if anyone there is interested in cashews from the liberated area of Mozambique or other such delights, we may have some information on it. Send anything—I'll read it all!

I hear that you're all going to become proud moms and dads or aunts and uncles—happy baby to Margaret. A hug to Jim, and yes, Keith, I am finally eating breakfasts, although I don't really enjoy them. Assorted love to everyone.

> Co-operatively and peacefully,
> Jan (deep in the heart of Lotus Land, BC)

P.S. Oh, Bill and I met Peruvian Paul just sleazing down Hastings Street one day. Many joints later… Bill is probably going to quit work soon—he's getting bushed tree planting up there in Scrambled River. I bump into a person a day from Waterloo! What are they all doing out here?

LEMON SESAME SQUARES
— Beth Brenneman, *Waterloo Food Co-op* newsletter

Base:

¾ cup vegetable oil

½ cup raw sugar or honey to taste

1¾ cups whole-wheat flour (or substitute ½ cup wheat germ for the flour)

1 tsp. salt

1½ cups rolled oats

Blend well and press into a 9 x 13 pan.

Topping:

2 eggs (turkey eggs sold at the co-op work just fine)

1 tsp. grated lemon peel★

2 Tbsp. lemon juice

½ tsp. salt

1 cup coconut

1 cup chopped nuts

1 cup raisins and/or currants

1 cup sesame seeds

Directions:

Mix, then spread over base. Bake at 350°F for at least 30 minutes or until top is set.

★*If anyone can suggest a substitute for the lemon peel that gives the same zing, let me know. I realize the peel has been sprayed and dyed and is unsafe for human consumption, but it really makes the difference between a bland nothingness and a great taste.*

Chapter 4

"MONEY, MONEY, MONEY"

At the end of 1975 the CRS Workers' Co-op included the following four projects: the cannery, with Ros and Roger as the primary workers; the co-op storefront coordinators, Dana and Gail; the Brokerage Collective; and Queenright, the beekeeping collective, with several workers.

Democratic management meant meetings—lots of them—to connect with others in the co-op and thrash out the issues of the day. Meeting attendance was mandatory and necessary to keep a handle on progress. Because we were funded by a job creation grant, the government guys would sit in sometimes just to see how things were going. On one occasion the government rep was a forty-something woman dressed in heels, a fashionable suit and makeup, a costume unfamiliar to the women of CRS. She sat among us and took notes. There were a few items of business that we did not want to have repeated in the government reports—just little things that might unduly influence them into cutting off funding. And there was one big thing: our method of capitalization. We talked nervously around the subject while the government rep continued to write—until she looked up with a smile and informed us that she was not writing damning judgments but only making out her shopping list.

In fact, CRS overcame the lack of capital funding in a unique way. Our monthly salaries and some expenses were provided by the federal funding grant. In the 1970s, there existed a regular alphabet soup of programs: OFY (Opportunities For Youth), LIP (Local Initiative Projects) and the one we were enrolled in, LEAP (Local Employment Assistance Program)—all of them offered in the hope of creating sustainable jobs. Why the feds were giving away so much money during that period is still a subject for speculation. We had decided that it was to keep us occupied and deter us from other radical activism.

The year 1970 had ended in a crisis in Canada when members of the Front de Libération du Québec (FLQ) kidnapped provincial cabinet minister Pierre Laporte and British diplomat James Cross. The Pierre Trudeau government invoked the War Measures Act, which granted powers to police for the arbitrary detention and arrest of anyone, especially hippies, activists or those under the age of thirty, whether involved with terrorist acts or not. Thus, the subsequent grant funding for job creation was considered a sop—it would keep us off the streets and engaged in useful pursuits. We would be managed by bureaucrats and perhaps create a few jobs along the way that would make the government's employment figures look good. The money was easily available. In an interview years later, Paul Phillips summed it up succinctly: "You could pick up the world and run with it," he recalled fondly.

Social activism continued to flourish side by side with the development of innovative workplaces such as ours. Were we being bought off? Probably, but it sure was good to make a living from work that felt useful and responsible.

We CRS members lived cheaply—usually in shared homes. None of us had children to support at that time, we rarely travelled except on co-op business, and only three members owned vehicles. Dana and Ros drove economical and road-weary Austins, and Gail owned a green Volkswagen Beetle convertible. Our groceries were purchased through the East End Food Co-op that CRS members, specifically Dana and Gail, had helped to set up.

Given this frugal lifestyle, we could afford to return part of our salaries each month into a fund that we controlled. These donations to the cause, which we called "kickbacks," were not monitored by the government or by any one person in the collective; it was up to each individual to deposit the funds into the CRS bank account. If a person needed to keep a little more personal money one month, he or she didn't donate. We learned later that the administrators of our funding, who kept a close bureaucratic eye on us, knew that we practised this method of capitalization. However, they seemed interested in our ingenuity, and we were likely the subject of their coffee break chat.

At the end of the first year of the grant, 1974, Dana recalls that CRS made it very clear to the funders that we could not be self-sufficient at the end of the three-year project if they did not allow us to retain earnings to capitalize our business. "We would have had to give surplus back to the government," he said, "instead of using it to grow the business." Dana and other members fought with the government for the first year over this issue and found some support from several of the project officers, including Phil Lyons and Michael Goldberg. "By 1975 we had acknowledgement and some respect," Dana said, "for taking only subsistence wages and kicking money back into the co-op."

The Brokerage Collective was the food-wholesaling arm of CRS, and it was struggling to be born, mostly through the efforts of a lone worker, Paul Newman, who had suffered numerous inane comments because he bore the same name as the famous actor. He had joined the CRS group shortly before me. He had carrot-red hair down to his waist, wore sloppy jeans and wanted to work for the revolution. His family had emigrated from California; his mother, Virginia, and father, Ray, were pacifists, concerned about America's gun culture, the threat of nuclear annihilation and the Vietnam War. When Paul's older brother had to register for the draft, they decided to whisk their two boys off to Canada before they could be called up. Paul lived for a few years on Salt Spring Island, where he played in a rock/roots band called the Sodbusters, and he continued to love and play music—a double bass and later the button accordion—throughout his time in CRS.

The goal of the Brokerage Collective was to research potential suppliers of the highest volume items, such as nuts and cheese—items preferred by the co-ops who ordered from Fed Up. We would negotiate to order these goods in bulk, either in sacks or case lots, thus allowing us the economies of scale for greater discounts on the price.

As the wholesaler evolved, numerous explanations were necessary to define our workplace and explain that we were not a Canada Customs brokerage. Most people didn't understand what exactly we did every day. I'm not sure we did ourselves. (Nonetheless, this CRS project developed many years later into one of the most important parts of the workers' co-op, eventually becoming Horizon Distributors.)

Our lack of experience in running a business was easily overcome by our dedication to learning as much as we could about the food products we were making or selling. We bent the ear of every potential supplier that we researched. It became our habit in the Brokerage Collective to always have two people on the line for every phone call. When one tired of asking questions, the other would chime in: What farming methods do your sources use? What does "*nonpareil* almonds" mean? How can we buy honey from the Peace River? What are the working conditions for your factory employees?

On more than one occasion we phoned a clerk at the Purchasing Commission, a provincial government department responsible for buying goods for use on BC Ferries. In this case we were simply gathering information on how to sell goods to a larger market. We wanted to buy a product in bulk—honey or flour, perhaps—something that the co-ops would want as well. We would submit our bid to provide ingredients to the Commission, thus assuring ourselves of at least one big market for our goods, and the co-ops would receive the economic benefit of the bulk buy. It was a clever plan and showed we were thinking like the big boys, even though nothing came of this effort, unless you count the offer of a recipe for clam chowder, the ubiquitous soup of BC Ferries.

We wrote down the answers to our many questions and shared them with the CRS group at our meetings. They shared their knowledge with us. While there was no reason for me to learn the pros and cons of overwintering bees or how to build a bee box (hive), I learned much about that from our Queenright Collective. There was definitely no delight in my camp to learn how to balance a chequebook or read a bottom line, but it was essential that everyone learned the basics of bookkeeping. This knowledge was a necessary component of democratic management. There were no bosses—we were all managers who needed to know every aspect of the business. I was continually struck by how little of this vital knowledge we had learned in school. CRS Workers' Co-op became my school.

Many of us had received a higher education: I had my knowledge of Russian literature, which did not serve me well in the food business, while Dana was a phi beta kappa who had studied creative writing. Gail had a degree in social work. Paul Newman had no post-secondary education

Paul Newman and Dana Weber learn bookkeeping from a patient Dick McGinnis (centre).

but was always the first to look up interesting facts in the encyclopedia and talk about them to whoever would listen. Later, he would be the first of the group to embrace the new field of computer technology.

As for the others, I couldn't say whether they had an academic education—it wasn't really important. Members were far more valuable to the group if they understood how to facilitate a meeting, negotiate a bargain price, use a pipe wrench or calculate the weight of an order. I had been educated in none of these things, but I learned fast. Gail commented in a 2016 interview that we weren't anti-intellectual: "We were being practical, trying to make something happen."

We also wanted to practise collective decision making, and we wanted to support other co-ops who had a venerable history of growth, such as the Fraser Valley Milk Producers or the Wheat Pool. We read up on their stories—how the little guys, the farmers, had banded together with other farmers to get a fair price for their goods. It sounded sensible to us. And if grassroots organizations such as the Wheat Pool had become just like the other big-guy corporations, well, that was because co-operatives were islands in a sea of capitalism. It was difficult to live on that economic island when everyone around us was grubbing for dollars. However, we

Ron Pither and Anne Williams grapple with bookkeeping for Queenright by learning from Dick McGinnis.

noted our advantage—we owned our island, and ownership is a powerful thing.

We looked to examples that have certainly fallen from favour today, particularly those from the People's Republic of China. We read from Mao Tse-tung's little books: *Be Concerned with the Well-being of the Masses*, *Pay Attention to Methods of Work* and *Combat Liberalism*. "Let a hundred flowers bloom," Mao announced in 1956. "Let a hundred schools of thought contend." We did not read his words as witless politicos slavishly following a dogma. We read thoughtfully and discussed them. In 1963 Mao asked, *Where Do Correct Ideas Come From?* in a propaganda pamphlet that was published in English. Ultimately they come from social practice, he advised, and this was our belief too. You practise what you preach. Once these ideas are grasped by the masses, he went on, they turn into a material force that changes society and changes the world. These concepts—the very basis of social activism—don't seem out of place today. It's unfortunate that we didn't know what was truly happening in China during the Cultural Revolution, when millions were harassed, humiliated, tortured and executed in terrifying purges. The cold-war propaganda that found its way to Vancouver spoke of only the positive aspects: the Chinese struggle for freedom from feudalism and imperialism and the dream of a classless society where women were equal to men. We admired the barefoot doctors who travelled into rural areas to provide health care and the sacrificing labours of the workers to build industry in China. We took the good and left the bad, or so we thought.

Some members also read George Orwell's *Homage to Catalonia* while flirting with anarchy, or they met to discuss author Marge Piercy's dystopian novel *Woman on the Edge of Time*. Others read the *Mother Earth News* or a treatise on worker self-management from Yugoslavian economist Branko Horvat. Could we learn from all of these sources? Yes.

Because it was the 1970s, we used what tools we had read or heard about within our community culture. Before each meeting we took a few moments—sometimes stretching into half an hour—for "shared appreciations and held resentments," to clear the air. Some in the group noted, with a frown, that this was "a bit touchy-feely," but nonetheless it served its purpose—sometimes. Other times the meetings bogged down in rhetoric and argument. We should sell widgets, said person X. We can't sell those because they are not environmentally and/or politically correct, said person Y. We should sell what the customers want, said person Z, in order to make money this month.

Ah, the bottom line. The famous co-operative double bottom line: we were not only looking at how many dollars we had taken in, but at what social value we had earned. Had we built a more equitable way of doing business? Had we fought racism and sexism? Had we advanced the redistribution of wealth?

For us profit was not called profit; it was known as surplus. We followed the co-operative principles, also known as the Rochdale Principles, named after a group of nineteenth-century workers in Rochdale, England. In one of their fundamental co-operative principles, it was required that surplus be ploughed back into the business to make it grow or to provide members with a dividend. In our case it was the former rather than the latter.

During the early years CRS had hired an accountant, Dick McGinnis, who proved to be a supportive teacher. Several of the group learned to do bookkeeping to trial balance from him, and the one co-op-owned adding machine with its spool of paper tape was kept busy. Financials were presented at each meeting and explained for the numerically challenged.

There was always a facilitator in the chair so that the often energetic and loud meetings could actually accomplish work. Note that I used the word "work." We weren't playing; we were serious about our worker-owned business. Perhaps too serious. It was difficult to laugh at ourselves, and we strived with some arrogance to show by example that we were on the right path. Other co-ops—of which there were many in the 1970s, forming the phenomenon known as the new-wave co-ops—were more "hippy dippy" than we were. We developed a reputation for being political and somewhat lacking in a sense of humour—though this was not how we saw ourselves. In our view we were taking the high ground. Some people, such as those managing Fed Up, the food co-ops' central depot, made good-natured jokes about us and chose a more laid-back style of management.

"We had our own agenda," Dana admitted years later. "We were trying to lead, but we didn't want to acknowledge that, since in co-ops we were all equal."

After much deliberation between all of the member co-ops at Fed Up council meetings, the organization decided to hire paid workers to manage the warehouse. Three people became the first unoriginally titled Paid Collective. One of them was Keith Jardine, who would continue to work on behalf of co-operatives and credit unions for many years. Another early member of the PC was Darcy Hamilton, who worked at Fed Up for years before becoming a member of Wild West Organic Harvest, another co-operative wholesaling endeavour that supplied fresh produce for the health food and co-op markets.

Because Fed Up was managed by all of its member-run co-ops, each co-op was required to send one or two workers to Vancouver for at least two weeks per year, and they would earn minor discounts on food.

The Paid Collective staff members were in place to oversee operations, but Fed Up's decision-making process rested squarely with a steering committee of members and the member co-ops themselves, who had the right and the obligation to participate. Those who came on work weeks would do warehouse work: receive orders from suppliers, pack orders for distribution to other member co-ops, clean the warehouse, participate in meetings and have great lunches together. In hindsight this was a clever idea, because every worker experienced ownership of the organization, and it gave them insight into food production and distribution. Also, it was great for meeting people. Joe from Smithers met Nancy from the Kootenays and both of them learned where their organic millet was grown and how to cut rounds of cheese for the least amount of wastage. Today we call it networking.

It was these Fed Up work weeks that had drawn people like Paul Newman into CRS. Living on Salt Spring Island and being a founding member of their rural food co-op, Paul had become enamored of Fed

Early days of the East End Food Co-op with Gail Cryer and Roger Inman behind the counter. Each co-op shopper and member was required to spend a few hours as volunteer help at the store.

Up's concept and volunteered for extra work weeks so he could visit the city. "We were hippies in those days," he remembers, "but also working Joes and Josephines too." After he got to know Paul Phillips, Ros and Dana through Fed Up, Paul made the permanent move to Vancouver in February of 1975.

Work in the Fed Up warehouse was loosely supervised by a rotating co-ordinator or "rotcor"—someone from a member co-op who took on the task of co-ordinating the duties of the visiting workers.

"You should do that," said Ros one day, showing me a copy of Fed Up's newspaper, the *The Catalist,* which had published an article seeking rotcor volunteers. I lacked the basic background in Fed Up's management to know how to direct others, so I agreed that instead I would go for a work week. My Fed Up experience would help me in the brokerage, I thought. It turned out to be a pivotal experience and one that, I later realized, was exactly the kind of productive grunt work that I had envisioned co-ops doing when I lived in Ontario. I lifted sacks of grains to fill orders, I swept the floor, I received deliveries, and I took part in a meeting of all the work week people to determine what new items should go into the catalogue.

"Can we have dish brushes with wooden handles instead of plastic?" asked one volunteer. Another was concerned that the nutritional yeast was not as good as the brewer's yeast previously supplied, although she was shouted down by those who maintained that it was more or less the same substance under a different name. These decisions sound trivial, though we took them seriously, but the real value was in meeting other like-minded people and forming relationships that would last into the next decade.

Chapter 5

GOING FOR BROKE

The Brokerage Collective spent its first few formative months in the autumn of 1975 working out of CRS's rundown house at 2141 Pandora Street in Vancouver. Two of the CRS founders, Dana and Ros, lived in the house. Dana's bedroom had its walls and ceiling plastered in aluminum foil by the previous occupant, and Ros's bedroom faced onto a drab apartment building. The basement offered another dingy bedroom that was used by a flock of Canada World Youth kids from Quebec, who must have been selected for this particular billet because of their adventurous spirits (although one young man complained that the room was too cold for his guitar).

The Pandora office was on the main floor in what had once been the dining room. Its furniture consisted of a wooden desk with a Selectric typewriter on it, a steno chair and a bookcase. On the wall were mounted all manner of posters and a blackboard covered in humorous notes and serious plans. A map of the world allowed us to look up changes in geography brought about by revolutionary activity in China and Africa.

And perched atop a filing cabinet was a framed photograph of some slick, wavy-haired movie star guy smiled down at us. Rumour has it that Ron Pither found the picture in the dumpster and signed it as Grant Rationale. This was our little joke, since we were funded by various federal government grants at the time, but coming up with a rationale for our goals that resonated with the feds was not a joke and was necessary in order for them to give us more money.

Other members of CRS lived at a house at 1868 Franklin Street, about three blocks from our "head office" on Pandora. This heritage home was surrounded by autobody shops on three sides, and the fourth side sported a wide, ramshackle verandah that looked out over an industrial building and in the distance to Burrard Inlet. On windy days putrid fumes from the chicken factory on Powell Street filled the air—that is, when they were not overwhelmed by the stench of motor fluids. Because of the house's vintage, the bathroom had been added as an afterthought at the back of the house, making it chilly in winter, as it did not receive the benefit of the coal furnace. The electrical circuits were also vintage and required glass fuses, which were becoming difficult to find. Nonetheless the house had some useful features: five bedrooms upstairs, a large kitchen with a pantry and a living room big enough for collective meetings. The rent was cheap.

CRS championed the rights of people to eat wholesome, good food, and we were directly opposed to the growth of agribusiness that was gobbling up so many small farmers and producers. These days information about good nutrition is better disseminated, and even fast-food chains have been urged by their customers to offer healthier menu items. More importantly, the principle of eating better is

(Top) The house at 2141 Pandora Street was the first office space for the Brokerage Collective. Dana Weber and Ros Breckner lived in the house.

(Bottom) Ah, "Grant Rationale." You were an inspiration and our little joke.

interwoven with the environmentally sound use of our planet. It seems strange to remember that no one was connecting the dots in the 1970s, except, that is, Frances Moore Lappé, whose paradigm-altering book, *Diet for a Small Planet,* had been published in 1971.

In the fall of 1975, when I joined the Brokerage Collective, Paul Newman had been working by himself for many months, grappling with how to set up the business of a food wholesaler. What role would we fulfill? We thought it would be a way to buy bulk foods cheaper and serve the smaller co-ops who could not afford the quantities of scale. But what would we sell? Organic foods? They were still a novelty at that time, sold mostly in health food stores and purchased by hippies. Or would

Office work is on the agenda for Paul Newman of the Brokerage Collective.

we sell foods from politically correct countries? But how would we define which countries could be trusted? South Africa was out of the running—that was for sure because of its apartheid policies—but what about African countries such as Tanzania that had considerable co-operative development?

And importantly, how would we differ from Fed Up, a collective that already operated a central depot to sell to other small food co-ops? The Fed Up coordinators asked us that question many times, but it took us years to come up with an answer. Obviously we needed to find our role by doing it.

We wrote numerous letters to addresses around the globe to ask, for example, whether we could acquire cashews from the liberated areas of Mozambique or if we could buy cocoa powder that had not been treated with alkali. We rarely received a reply, so we made slow progress. The value of organic food had already been given a boost by the two friends of the cannery, Lee and Bob McFadyen in Cawston, BC, and they were enthusiastic and vocal cheerleaders among farmers in their area. They gave us an earful on the importance of promoting organic; we developed contacts from them. The terms "agri-business" and "whole foods" became part of our vocabulary.

Then Robin Lett joined us, bringing with her an enthusiasm for organically grown grains and produce. She had previously volunteered to find sources of organic goods in Canada for Marginal Market, a retail co-op near Granville Street, and she had established connections with the very few prairie farmers who strived to grow crops in a healthy way. We learned about organic certification in Canada—or the lack of it. In 1972 the International Federation of Organic Agriculture Movements was founded, but regulations for the organic certification of farmers' fields took years to develop—in fact, the first definition of "organic" published in the Food Labelling Guidelines of Consumer and Corporate Affairs was not determined until 1989. We learned that organically grown food differed from unsprayed fruit and vegetables. Some farmers might practise the latter on their way to organic conversion, whereas others might truthfully label their produce unsprayed when they were still using synthetic fertilizers in the soil. Such produce had to be priced higher than supermarket goods since it took more rigorous work on the part of the farmer/gardener to grow organically.

Robin knew a lot about Canada's politics and claimed to be from Saskatchewan, although she spoke with a Chicago accent. She always wore her frizzy red hair wrapped in a bandana that was pulled down over her forehead. As I was learning to be more curious and ask more questions, I asked her about the ever-present kerchief. She replied that it was because she dyed her hair and didn't want anyone to see the black roots. This was strange, since none of the other co-op women were concerned about hair colour. We did not wear makeup and we never bothered to dress in anything more than utilitarian clothes.

She didn't last long with the Brokerage Collective, but her contribution was significant since she turned our focus toward the burgeoning natural foods market. Years later, when the US announced an amnesty on political refugees who had fled to Canada, Robin returned to her homeland in the States, bandana-free, to be accountable for her earlier role in a militant activist organization.

While CRS members still ate meat, we were becoming aware of how raising cattle was putting a burden on land use. A few chickens could produce food for many by grazing a small patch of soil, while cows ate up the resources and provided food for only a few. Sometimes we ate lunch or dinner together at the Pandora Street house—cheap food, but wholesome: herring from a tin, rice and beans, spaghetti, and fat old hens in the stew pot.

However, Dana was a good cook who would often challenge himself to produce more elaborate dishes for special dinners. He used recipes that took all day to prepare with a multitude of ingredients: salmon *koulibiaka*, spanakopita, Black Forest cake with kirsch liqueur and *obst* torte, which was made by grinding nuts laboriously by hand in a Mouli grater.

"I wonder how Dana will cope after the revolution without his grater," mused Paul one day. Fortunately, Dana did not hear the comment, and it was noteworthy that Paul was often first to the table to eat Dana's creations. We could already see that there was a great future for Dana in a bakery—a worker-owned bakery, of course.

Meanwhile, Paul continued to think big on behalf of the brokerage, poring over a catalogue from China that offered utilitarian trucks for export. They were stark in their simplicity, and he noted that though they had heaters and windshield wipers, not one had an AM/FM radio, an eight-track or even chromies. We did not order one—it seemed too big a project, and besides, it would have looked out of place among the souped-up Detroit machines and choppers that our neighbours parked on Pandora Street. Paul also placed a survey in the Fed Up newspaper, asking members if they wanted the Brokerage Collective to supply coffee beans from a fairly traded source. They did—but that venture would not happen until 1976.

At first I tagged along behind him on our supplier research jaunts, feeling useless. What did I know of the grocery business? But I learned quickly. We visited a nut supplier in Burnaby, and we went by bus to Victoria to meet with the People's Share Collective, granola makers to the co-op movement.

On one memorable occasion, we invited a man from Chile to the Pandora Street office to tell us why we should not boycott that country, even during its dictatorship years. It harms the growers and producers,

The Brokerage Collective spread its supplier research far and wide, from beans grown in Manitoba to coffee from Papua New Guinea.

he told us, without adversely affecting the ruling junta. This question of boycotts was a subject for CRS meetings on several occasions and was particularly pertinent to the food wholesaler, since we had to take into account the politics and practices of major suppliers. Several of the group had considered our Chilean visitor to be a CIA operative—paranoia was still rampant in Canada at that time. We all remembered the 1970 War Measures Act, with its sweeping powers for the RCMP and its subsequent raids on every left-leaning group or publication in Vancouver, regardless of whether they were considered subversive or not. We were vulnerable. We knew that our grant funders could easily shut us down and that access to money to keep the projects running was of primary importance. Some far-seeing members urged us to find ways to control and administer our own funds without relying on government handouts. The banks were made of marble, as it is written in the lyrics of the labour union song, so Canada's national banking establishments were unlikely to care whether our small businesses thrived. Fortunately, the co-op movement possessed its own form of financial institution, founded by the people, for the people's well-being: the credit union.

Sometime that autumn Michael Goldstein showed up at the door of the office on Pandora Street with a sheaf of documents in hand. Several of the CRS members knew him as someone who had worked with co-operatives in a positive way, and he was now trying to organize a credit union, a financial institution that would serve co-ops and non-profits, those that the banks spurned as too small or too risky. This was right up our alley. It was to be called the Community Congress for Economic Change or CCEC Credit Union. He had already signed up several dedicated people as founders on a charter document to be submitted for incorporation, but he wanted more signatures. He found them among us. We passed the documents around and several expressed interest in serving on the new credit union's board of directors. Right on!—as we said in those days. This was what co-operatives needed: access to funds that were not governed by the big business of Canada's banks or subject to the day's political whims. The credit union movement would be a big boon to women in business as well, recognizing their abilities to manage a loan without requiring a man at the helm.

However, there was a big gap between the time that CCEC's documents were signed and the credit union received its charter on February 2, 1976, after which it was allowed to open its doors. It briefly occupied a location at 207 West Hastings Street. At first it could not provide chequing services, so we continued to do our banking at Gulf and Fraser Fishermen's Credit Union, another grassroots financial institution. Most of us opened our personal share/savings accounts at CCEC when it moved to its first real office at 205 East Sixth Avenue. I was member number 32 and my deposit card reports that on March 4, 1976, I deposited four dollars to open my account, after which the deposits and withdrawals continued sporadically until 1981. That first transaction was initialled by K, which probably stood for Katherine Ruffen, the first manager.

The best thing about this credit union was its personal service in the days before ATM machines. If I had neglected to withdraw cash on a Friday for the weekend's activities, I could call Katherine at work and tell her I was on my way. "Please don't leave until I get there," I would say, and I would arrive minutes before closing time. It's doubtful whether any bank or credit union today would be concerned about my lack of cash for the weekend.

Chapter 6

BEEKEEPERS AND STOREKEEPERS

After the cannery began production in June 1975, Floyd returned to his other role at CRS's Queenright, the beekeeping collective. Though this group had incorporated as a producers' co-op separately from CRS, the collective was still considered part of the CRS industries and its members participated in meetings of the whole. They operated from a woodworking shop on industrial East Hastings Street, in a dusty basement—far removed from pastoral beehives—in which they built wooden bee boxes and kept in touch with those up north who cared for Queenright's bees in summer, a two-hundred-colony apiary with honey production destined for Fed Up's member co-ops. The bees were then trucked to Vancouver to overwinter in a warmer climate, a practice not common among commercial beekeepers in those days, since most were inclined to kill the season's bees and start fresh in the spring. Queenright also had aspirations to develop a local queen-rearing industry to supply beekeepers with good-quality queens at a reasonable price.

The key to Queenright's operation was its founder, Ron Pither, the public face of the beekeeping co-op. "Pollination for the Nation" was the slogan of the day. He had considerable experience as an apiarist at his home on Mayne Island, making him valuable to the group. He had first learned about bees from Jimmy Lindow, who taught beekeeping at a free university and had organized a project called Busy Bees that was concerned with queen rearing. By 1975 Jimmy had also come to work at Queenright with Ron and Floyd.

Ron recalls Jimmy as a "fussbudget about accuracy," but he says he learned much about bees from the older man. Other beekeepers soon became part of the group: Phil Laflamme, Sig Steiner and Anne Williams. Later, Gerda Osteneck joined them in the woodworking shop. All were dedicated to the hives and all brought talent to the group.

The Queenright Beekeeping Co-op operated a woodworking shop in Vancouver where the members made bee boxes. Someone from the collective must have made this delightful sign.

In a journal, *BC Alternative*, published in 1974, Queenright's organizers outlined many of its dreams for fostering beekeeping. Not all of the dreams came to reality, but the collective was dedicated to their cause. "When you're a beekeeper, you're happy in the bee yard," Ron said. "It's a magical relationship with insects, with other life forms."

Ron and some of his buddies, including the plumber, Al Poole, and a beekeeping poet from Powell River named Murray Kennedy, organized a softball team called The Flex Morgan Mock Heroics, who played for fun in the early 1970s. One day after a game, Murray was knocked into a solid concrete pillar—resulting in a concussion. He went into a coma so severe that many thought he would not emerge. Eventually he became responsive enough that he could signal yes or no with his eyes such that when Ron visited him in hospital, Murray could answer Ron's big question: "Do you want me to bring the bees?" After Murray blinked "yes," Ron immediately went home to fetch a glass observation hive that had been used in schools to teach kids about bees. He returned to the hospital, whisking this hive full of bees past the nurses with great speed before they could complain, and positioning it where Murray could see it.

"The bees healed him," Ron contends to this day. Although he had a brain injury, Murray was able to return to most of his activities, including softball.

Anne Williams gets down to work for Queenright while Ron Pither exults.

The bee workers of Queenright kept their hives up north.

The East End Storefront Co-op, as it was first called, opened in early 1975. The store was located at 1806 Victoria Drive in its early years and was no bigger than any other corner grocery store, but we members were very proud of it. Later its title was streamlined to East End Food Co-op, and at the time of this writing it is still in existence in Vancouver, though now on Commercial Drive.

The idea was to convert from a prepay, pre-order system to a stocked store. In order to start up, Gail and Dana from CRS, the storefront co-ordinators, determined that to have a successful store they would need 240 member households to commit. Consequently the credit union account bore the name 240 Storekeepers.

The co-op was member-run, though its members hired a part-time paid co-ordinator to provide consistency and oversee the store's operation, and each member was expected to share the work as a volunteer by signing up for a shift cutting cheese, unpacking cartons of apples or working the cash register. Among its goals was to know more about the food we were eating, where it came from and its nutritional value. The co-op also wanted to support local producers who were, according to a

An early incarnation of the East End Co-op Storefront found its first home on Victoria Drive, Vancouver. It later moved to Commercial Drive.

co-op brochure written in 1980 or 1981, "under pressure from monopolies and cheap import food." Shopping at the co-op was a sociable activity, a place to meet friends and chat about politics or the weather, even if sometimes the conversation turned to complaints about, for example, the quality of the tomatoes: "Zey are all ze time ugly," complained one francophone shopper. Or gripes from the co-ordinator about members not showing up for their work shifts. Several of these co-ordinators came and went over the period from 1975 through 1980 while the store's financial health ebbed and flowed.

I sat on the East End's board of directors and became immersed in the day-to-day problems of a small grocery store. I also volunteered for an extra duty—that of painting the store's concrete floor with a new coat of red paint that would look cleaner and brighten up the place. Another member, Penny, and I began our work early on a day that the store was closed and discovered that the paint that had been purchased for us was a durable, oil-based paint that would not wash off our rollers in the sink as we had hoped. The paint gave off a pungent industrial odour, and we were light-headed from the fumes by the time we finished our duties.

"We'll have to take the rollers and brushes back home and clean them in the laundry tub there," I told Penny, thus dooming the interior of my home's concrete laundry tub to a lifetime of colourful red designs. Still, the store's floor was painted and everyone was bound to be happy with the improvement. That's what we thought, anyway, until we received an irate phone call from the co-ordinator the next day.

"The cheese stinks of paint!" she shouted with no preamble. "Why didn't you cover it? I have to throw it out—that's a huge loss of money!" Apparently the stench of the paint had seeped right through the plastic wrap on the cut-up wedges of cheese in the cooler. The smell was also to be found lingering in some of the produce that had been carefully covered, and it had even permeated the back room, the co-ordinator's lair. Rather than being thanked for our labours, we had to apologize and bear the blame for the co-op's loss. I think my household even bought some of the smelly cheese, at a discount of course, to relieve my guilt.

Chapter 7

MS. CHEESE AND HONEY

Sometime toward the end of 1975, the residents of Pandora Street moved to a more comfortable home on Woodland near First Avenue. Here Paul and I could spread out in our new office in the finished basement—and do some real work.

Gerry Dragomir joined the Brokerage Collective at that time. He was a short, slight, bespectacled man with an interest in the financial end of the operation. His involvement in CRS had started before mine, dating back to when he lived in Victoria. Though he had trained as a law clerk, he had been unemployed and was shopping at the Amor de Cosmos food co-op. His girlfriend, Sheila Adams, was attending the University of Victoria. At that time Ros, Dana and Paul Phillips had provided background and help with resources in Victoria in the organization of an urban-style storefront food co-op, Fernwood, which flourished for many years. When Gerry saw the work that was being done on the various CRS projects, including Fernwood, he recalls being very enthusiastic, and he moved to Vancouver and into the ramshackle house on Franklin Street. Soon after, Sheila joined him to work with CRS.

Together they worked on setting up the Fed Up newsletter, later designated a genuine newspaper and named *The Catalist*. It was a very useful means of communication within the co-op movement, as its newsprint pages contained informative articles, rants, letters, news about the pre-order co-ops across the province, minutes from Fed Up council meetings and the all-important, ever-present centrefold, which listed the catalogue of items sold through Fed Up.

Until Gerry joined the Brokerage Collective there had been a sense among the co-op members that it was spinning its wheels, simply gathering supplier information in a directionless manner, charmed by each new diversion, whether it was imported Chinese trucks or green coffee beans. But while it was true that the fields were fallow, they were also being enriched for growth. New values were shaping up: the need to sell organic whole food, the desire to support other co-ops and socially minded producers and, most importantly, the willingness to run a business in a non-hierarchical, non-sexist manner. No one was leader—although when necessary Ros, Dana or Gail often acted as spokesperson for the group. As a woman, I was an equal in the workers' co-op along with colleagues of either gender. "Women hold up half the sky," Mao had said. We took the words to heart.

It was important, then, that we not stereotype the only woman in the Brokerage Collective (me) by sentencing her to office work, so it was left to Gerry to make and field phone calls in a personable, chatty way—one salesman even gave up his prize-winning recipe for Cream of Lettuce Soup—while Paul and I searched for suitable warehouse space.

CREAM OF LETTUCE SOUP

Ingredients:

1 Tbsp. butter

2 cups green onion, chopped

2 sprigs parsley

2 cups soup stock

7 cups (or more) of torn lettuce, Swiss chard or other leafy green veggies

1 cup light cream or yogurt

1 tsp. salt

¼ tsp. pepper or paprika

1 tsp. tarragon

Directions:

Sauté the onions and parsley in butter melted in a large (4 quart or larger) saucepan. Stir in the lettuce and/or greens and stock and simmer for 25 minutes or until greens are tender. If a consistent thickness is desired, sieve or blend the soup and return to the saucepan. Add the cream or yogurt and spices, and either reheat or cool to serve (it's good both ways). This same recipe may be used to prepare a soup using asparagus in place of lettuce/greens.

We rented our first real warehouse at 1011 Commercial Drive. It was small, but it had the required loading dock for truck deliveries and there was room inside for a few pallets of our first offerings: sacks of alfalfa seed suitable for growing fresh sprouts, black turtle beans from Manitoba in fifty-kilogram sacks and canning jars from a manufacturer in Richmond, which we transported in a tiny Toyota truck borrowed from our poet acquaintance, Murray Kennedy. Now, there were many decisions to make, large and small: we needed a shop vac, a direct phone line and a catalogue of goods for sale.

But our first priority was to build a walk-in cooler, since we were expecting an order of cheese from Ontario. Gerry studied up on refrigeration, and Paul framed in the cooler while I assisted somewhat uselessly and added terminology to my vocabulary: "compressor" and "chill factor." Another worker was drafted into procuring and placing batts of fibreglass in our crude structure. The important thing was that it worked, though it was not completed in time for our first order of cheese.

That first delivery had to come to Fed Up's warehouse, and I was on hand to receive it; it was to be ripe, tasty Ontario cheddar. I arrived early at the Fed Up office and paced the floor of the warehouse until the driver finally showed up—late.

"Where do you want this shipment of German butter cheese?" he asked me. Spotting the panic on my face, he snorted with laughter and admitted that it was cheddar.

This cheese was my baby. When I had visited my parents in Toronto during the winter of 1975/76, I had taken the time, much to their consternation, to travel around southern Ontario through frost and snow with an old friend from my former communal house, a laid-back guy named Keith Wallace. He believed in co-ops and threw himself into this supplier research project with enthusiasm. (Later he went into the organic juice business, founding Black River Juice.) We set out in Keith's van to visit many of the small dairy farmers and their cheese plants dotted around the countryside, because I was convinced that the cheese was better here than in BC—richer, tangier. It made your sinuses sweat like a good cheese should.

Keith Wallace was my cheese-research colleague and friend. This photo was taken as he made deliveries to co-ops in southern Ontario. After working with co-ops for most of his career he started up the Black River Juice business using local fruit.

At one of the places we visited, the Central Manufacturing Cheese and Butter Co-op, the plant workers had been up since six that morning and would continue to work until four that afternoon. This plant stayed open six days a week during the season. Ross, the cheese maker, jumped to the sound of the store bell, came out of the plant and ran to the counter. A creamy aroma of fresh milk filled the air, and over Ross's shoulder we could see workers in the plant operating giant paddles that ran the full length of a large horizontal stainless-steel holding tank. Beside the tank stood a pail of fresh curd to be sold in the store daily to the tourists, along with packages of whey butter—two by-products of the industry. We could see it was a relief for Ross to wait on a customer every so often as it gave him a chance to stop and chat or smoke a cigarette.

On the counter was a stack of magazines titled *Milk Producer*. In among the close-ups of infected cow teats and photos of a smiling Eugene Whelan, the minister of agriculture at that time, was a feature article on the selection of Miss Ontario Milk Producer for 1975. The lucky winner—a woman, not a cow as you might expect—graced the cover of this trade journal.

"Guess they figured they had to sell the magazine somehow," said Ross apologetically. "Take some home with you."

He took us on a private tour and we watched the stainless-steel churns separating the curds from the whey. We bit into fresh cheese curds, savouring their waxy, squeaky feel, and sampled white and orange cheddar, new and old, butter cheese, marble, brick and several specialty cheeses.

The tour was more than a lesson in dairy practices—it was an eye-opener that taught us about big-business monopolies, because the quotas of many of the small farmers were being bought out by Black Diamond or Kraft at that time. Some dairy farmers were relieved that they did not have to rely on the old-fashioned auction system known as a Dutch clock, in which their cheese could end up being sold to a low bidder at below the cost of producing it. But not all were happy. One of the farmers invited us in, sat us down in overstuffed chairs in his roomy kitchen and grumbled.

"Oh, they've all tried to buy us out—Kraft and so on—but we wouldn't be subdued," he told us. "I think we didn't know what we were getting into with the marketing board, and now we're losing our freedom." He rocked back and forth rhythmically on his chair and gazed out at the farmland. The room was stifling hot despite the cold, clear winter day outside. A saucer of freshly sliced old white cheddar sat on the table.

"That's some of my best—from last year's milk. Milk changes through the season. You'll get more cheese from the same amount of milk in November than you will in July. Don't know why—funny…"

All of his milk was heat-treated but not pasteurized, he explained, as he needed the heat treatment to breed the bacteria that ages the cheese.

"We used to breed the starter ourselves from the raw milk, but now we get it from the lab. Everyone does now. But it doesn't taste quite the same." His cheese plant was over one hundred years old. "I guess we know how to make cheese," he said.

A shaggy Labrador began to eye the plate of cheese speculatively. There was a small uproar when the dog aimed for a chunk and the dairy farmer's wife rushed into the kitchen to shoo him away. Keith and I took a piece of cheese and let it melt slowly in our mouths. The tang dimpled my palate and spread slowly up both sides of my nose—it was obviously good quality.

The man told us more about the factory he belonged to—a stock factory, he called it, which was owned by the dairy farmers. The farmer sold to the Milk Marketing Board and they sold the milk back to the cheese factory according to quota. The government took a profit at both ends, he grumbled, and the cheese plants couldn't get as much milk as they asked for.

"They say there's a cheese surplus, but no one really knows… It would be like some folks in Ottawa trying to run your outfit in Vancouver. How can they do it from far away? The MMB tells us what to do and the cheese producers' association voted to join the MMB, so I guess we're trapped now." He continued, "The majority of our cheese goes to the auction—it's supposed to, anyhow—but we sell some over the counter at $1.25 for new cheddar. Last time I got $1.06 a pound at the auction. Also I sell to Campbell's Soup in Chatham—never figured out what they want cheese for!"

Under the terms of the MMB, cheese makers were to take all their cheese to the government-regulated warehouse to store it and have it graded before the auction. The farmer had complied with this until he learned that the inspector was grading his cheese as a B, not the finest quality. When he complained, an inspector checked the government facilities and found that the staff was letting the cheese sit out of the cooler for days without proper temperature control.

"Well," he continued, "I'm darn well going to take all my cheese to the private warehouse from now on. That didn't stop them—they called me up in the night, threatening to have me arrested for not keeping to the regulations. You know, I'm thinking of loading up a truck full of cheese and just driving it across the country…selling it ourselves."

I continued to make notes as he rambled on. What he was saying sounded just like the farmers' issues with the tree fruit marketing board in BC. Sitting in that warm farmhouse kitchen that smelled faintly of sour milk, listening to him rant, we felt angry on his behalf. It was one of those epiphany moments for me that strengthened my conviction. I could see with clarity that the only thing we could do to help was to continue on exactly the path we had begun—buying from and supporting small producers.

While in Ontario, I located a good bargain—giant waxed rounds of cheddar at a low price from a small dairy. They could be shipped easily enough to Vancouver, but they would have to be cut up to be distributed to our markets. Even now, any time I smell vinegar, I remember that first season of sales in the new warehouse. We wore white jackets as we used a wire to cut the ninety-pound rounds into chunks; they were bathed in vinegar and water to prevent mold and packed into airtight plastic bags. Fed Up ordered them from us for resale to their pre-order co-ops, while several larger co-ops ordered full rounds directly. We were in business.

Gerry Dragomir had an aptitude for bookkeeping, and he quickly set up a one-write carbon copy cheque-writing and accounting system—a gift for a small business in the days before computers. He had previously taken some bookkeeping classes, but his real reason for offering to do the work was what he called "self-preservation."

"While we were in the downstairs office at Woodland Street," he recalls, "Dana was doing the books for the group upstairs. There was screaming and tantrums from him. It was such a tortured process that I finally went upstairs and said to Dana, 'Maybe I can help.' Peace reigned after that."

As the co-op grew, bookkeeping for CRS would become Gerry's sole job, but first the Brokerage Collective had to move to a bigger warehouse. In our search for the perfect size and rental price for a warehouse, Paul and I roamed the city. We must have appeared rather different from other business owners, Paul with his long hair and sagging jeans and me

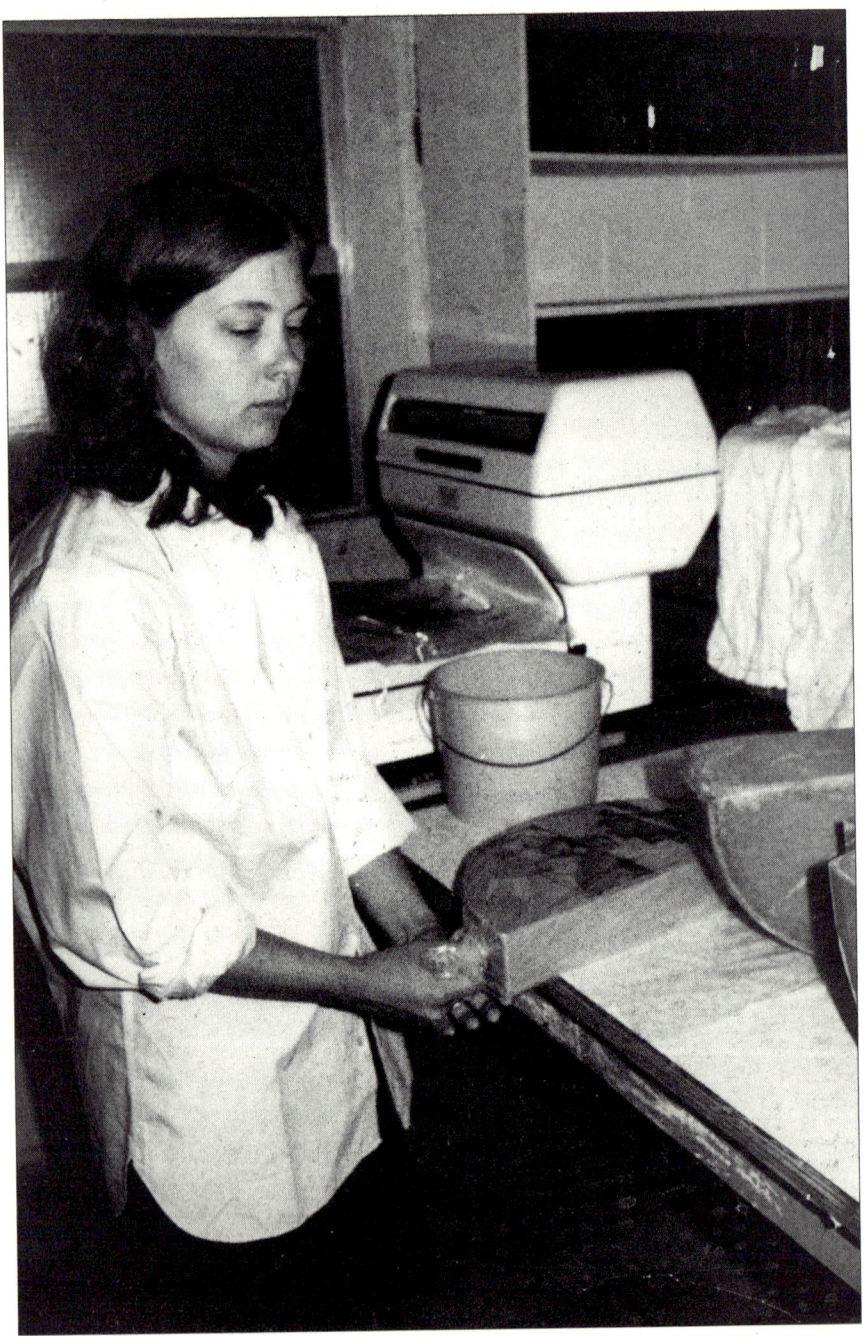

Portrait of the author as a young cheese cutter. The ninety-pound rounds had to be cut into wedges with a wire, bathed in vinegar and wrapped tightly before shipping to the co-ops.

with my plaid work shirt, as we asked weary building managers about access to railcar spurs so that we could bring in five tons of Canadian salt at a time by freight train from Ontario—another grand scheme that was never realized.

Finally we found the perfect place, a forty-five-hundred-square-foot warehouse at 4025 East Second Avenue near Boundary Road in Burnaby, and it was the coming of age for our wholesaling collective. Our new warehouse was big enough to also house the cannery, which was still in operation in North Vancouver at that time, so the canning equipment was moved into one corner of the warehouse, although much modification was needed. The building inspector scratched his head when he looked at our plans. He pointed out that we would need a trench in the concrete floor in order to drain off the liquids created in the steam kettles and that our use of sugar would erode the concrete over time. Smugly we informed him that we were using honey in our preserves; this was a new concept to him.

The health inspector was also thrown for a loop by the many hairy men and booted women who nonetheless kept such a clean warehouse. His advice was to warn of the one rat that he had seen crossing Lougheed Highway near our location. After several visits from this fellow, we discovered that the rat had been sighted over five years earlier and had never been seen since.

We rented a jackhammer to drill out a trench in the floor so that fluids could run downhill to the drain. This was cause for much excitement amongst both the cannery and the brokerage collectives, because we had never tried such a task before, and we each took a turn inserting earplugs and feeling our bones turn to jelly while using the giant tool. Fortunately, the warehouse concrete floor sloped naturally toward a drain, so day by day, the open trench moved toward this goal until the messy, noisy job was done. The trench was then covered by a grate that would allow us to drag pallet jacks over it.

With the new set-up of the cannery, we had to make several modifications to the small front office to allow for a heated lunchroom, and we were proud that everything fit together so "cosmically," as we said at the time. We considered ourselves strong and self-reliant.

We also had to get the wobbly toilet running efficiently. To my surprise I volunteered for this undesirable task, and wielding my pipe wrench in the approved fashion, I attacked the nuts that held the bowl in place. In a fit of zeal I swung my wrench too enthusiastically and cracked the vitreous porcelain—I later found out that vitreous means "china that has the properties of glass." Now no one could use the toilet, and I had to hastily find a new one at a used-parts yard and then figure out how to install it, much to my chagrin. But I had help with the installation from a new recruit—Malcolm. He was a summer student who didn't plan on staying, although he had told us that he wanted a career in the co-op movement. He sighed and clucked at my efforts, but he turned out to be very handy when it came to the final stage: placing a ring of wax on the floor, settling the bowl into position, then sitting on it to seal it.

The new warehouse already had a big walk-in cooler in which we could store many of the new products we had sourced: nuts, dried fruit, sunflower seeds, unfiltered apple cider and, of course, cheese. By that time our inventory included seven varieties of Canadian cheeses, including colby, feta, brick and caraway, as well as seven varieties of imported cheeses, including gouda, Danish blue, havarti and a smelly esrom wrapped in foil. When a vegetarian customer pointed out that the rennet used to curdle cheese was an animal product derived from the stomach of young ruminants such as calves, we researched a source of rennetless cheese. Another customer asked what was used as a dye in orange cheese. Interestingly, we discovered that it was not chemical food colouring; the dye came from the annatto seed, so it was vegetable based. Responding to these concerns was time-consuming but very educational.

Not all of our products met with success. We had ordered buckwheat from a supplier and then shipped out the unhulled grain to several co-ops in the north. One fellow wrote to us angrily to say that he had "boiled the bejesus out of the buckwheat" and it was still inedible. As a result we learned to ask even more questions of the suppliers of our many grains: buckwheat, millet, bulgur, barley and organic brown rice.

We stocked large white pails of Peace River honey, which was also my bailiwick, and I became known as Ms. Cheese and Honey—a role I loved, since they were everyone's favourite foods. I subscribed to a newsletter about honey that was published in Washington, DC, and learned interesting things about honey's relationship with water, its longevity and its health benefits. Honey absorbs moisture and odours from the air, so it must be kept covered, but it can keep for centuries, and ancient peoples were the first to understand its healing qualities. We visited the library or read pamphlets at the health food stores to find that only unadulterated, unpasteurized honey had antiseptic and antibacterial properties. However, the Peace River clover honey that we ordered was the real thing. We could also get malt-brown buckwheat honey for less cost, but most customers wanted clover. (For use at home, I loved the wildflower or fireweed honey because of its fragrance.)

When we began to buy it in 650-pound drums, it often came crystallized and it was necessary to strap an electric blanket (or honey warmer) around the barrel in order to make it liquid enough to flow into thirty-pound pails—a sticky job. We learned that when honey, which is initially liquid, crystallizes, it is only a sign that the glucose molecules are aligning in a natural process—it is not a sign of age or impurity.

There was one other thing we quickly learned about honey: it was slippery. When we finally had room to warehouse our pails of honey, Gerry Dragomir and Ron Pither set about transferring the buckets from their temporary home at Fed Up to the new warehouse. They used Ron's ancient flatbed truck, loaded the pails aboard and tied them with, as Gerry recalls, one piece of string. As the truck lumbered up the hill on Great Northern Way with Gerry in the driver's seat, he fervently hoped that they would make the left turn onto Clark Street without stopping at the traffic light. They didn't. Forced to stop on the hill, Gerry eased the clutch out when the light turned green again and gently moved the truck forward. Suddenly the clutch bucked, the truck lurched, and he could hear the *plop plop* of buckets of honey rolling off the flatbed and down the street, spilling their contents.

"I didn't realize how slippery honey was," he recalled, as he described how he saw the cars behind them sliding down the slope. "We got on the traffic report that night!" They scurried outside to pick up honey buckets as best they could, but in their retelling of the episode back at the office, they gave a nonchalant, no-harm-done account of the damage.

Our September 1976 catalogue covered two sides of white, legal-sized paper, and it was printed on a Gestetner machine. As I recall, I was the one who laboriously typed on purchased Gestetner stencil forms, using a great quantity of the pink, smelly liquid to cover mistakes. Photocopiers were available—it wasn't quite the dark ages of technology—but photocopies were expensive, whereas mimeographing by Gestetner was cheap.

The catalogue covered our limited inventory, featuring our first products, which included alfalfa seeds for sprouting, Tunnel Canary fruit, and black turtle beans. Canadian-produced cheese was a big seller, and we carried honey and bee pollen (considered a healthy supplement), which we obtained through Queenright. The black beans were a risky purchase because consumers were not familiar with them—but they were politically correct, as they were a wholesome Canadian-grown food. We wrote to the Manitoba Agricultural Products Marketing Commission for recipes and received some good ones, often complete with charming notes from the chef.

Fed Up's catalogue listed a few of the Brokerage Collective's items, including cheese and alfalfa seeds for sprouting.

BAKED BLACK BEANS

Ingredients:

2 cups black beans

6 cups water

⅓ cup molasses

2 Tbsp. dry mustard

4 Tbsp. honey

½ Tbsp. wine vinegar

2 oz. salt pork

1 package dry onion soup mix

½ Tbsp. lemon juice

Directions:

Put beans and water in covered pot and bring to a boil for 3 minutes. Remove from heat and allow to stand for 40 minutes. Boil again for 1 hour. Drain and save 2 cups of liquid. Mix other ingredients in the 2 cups of drained liquid. Place beans in covered bean pot or casserole dish. Add the 2 cups of mixed ingredients. Stir and place salt pork in centre of beans. Cook in the oven at 300 F for 4 hours, stirring every hour and adding water as required. Chef's note: Serve with thick slabs of fresh, hot buttered French bread and cold, sparkling white wine.

Chapter 8

WITH A LITTLE HELP FROM MY FRIENDS

Our dream was to become the food wholesaler to BC's co-operatives on the same scale as a similar group in the States, the Seattle Workers' Brigade (SWB), which had been founded in 1973 during an economic depression in Seattle, after the downsizing of the city's large employer, Boeing Aircraft. The SWB's wholesaling collectives were called CC Grains and Community Produce. Their giant warehouse near Seattle's port area, staffed mostly by women, wholesaled a huge variety of beans, seeds, rice, oils, dried fruit, juices and flours, and they were making deliveries across the border to co-ops and health food stores in Vancouver.

In 1976 the SWB decided to stop their Vancouver run—for what reason, I don't remember, but many of the foods they carried were not grown in Canada, and we would have had to import them to offer them to our markets. The Brokerage Collective agreed to take over this Vancouver business, and the SWB supplied us at a five percent markup.

The SWB was a role model for us. Paul had been in contact with Lara Morrisey, one of its founders, and she continued to support us in our new set-up. Her cheerful voice could be heard on the phone as she gave us the latest news about where they were buying their cashews, for example, and whether she could send a case of something our way. "I've got an LTL leaving on the 25th," she would say, "and could send you five to ten cases of R and Ts." This was code to say that their wholesaler was shipping a Less Than Load truck up north with an order, and there was room on board to supply us with Roasted and Tamaried mixed nuts. The information and the quality of the goods that came from America were excellent and gave us a big boost.

It was Lara who later told CRS about the New School for Democratic Management, a training program out of San Francisco that was coming to Seattle, where we could learn more about running our worker-managed businesses. During the latter years of the decade, several of us CRS members journeyed to Seattle to take part in courses that taught us better methods of financial and democratic management. Riding this huge learning curve was exactly what we needed in order to run the industries in a knowledgeable and professional manner. Plus there was the exhilarating advantage of meeting co-operators running businesses like our own and like-minded individuals working in the non-profit sector. While we learned from them, we made friends with many of the Americans and visited them in their homes.

I saved my notes from these workshops and they illustrate my concerns at that time. On my To Do list for when I returned to the co-op, I wrote, "Reorganize Accounts Payable to last possible date of payment" and "Do a break-even analysis." Though not exactly groundbreaking Harvard Business School material, these concepts were new to me. When the topic was marketing, I learned that: "The product will have no value if no one in the market values it." This was followed by a note in my handwriting: "black beans?" Obviously I had doubts as to whether the pallet of bean sacks in the warehouse would ever sell—and underneath I had added my further comment: "not a Marxist interpretation."

By 1980 we had decided to hold a similar series of training workshops in Vancouver, employing a few of the American instructors and inviting co-ops, community organizations and non-profit associations to learn in an ambient setting.

Community Business Training, the Vancouver session of the American program, was held in February 1980 at Capilano College's downtown campus, an ugly, concrete, wheelchair-inaccessible building situated on the Howe Street speedway. That didn't stop a satisfying turnout of students from various local co-ops eager to learn more. Courses offered included: Accounting, Marketing, Planning, and the most popular one, Democratic Management. Joan Makaroff, a CRS member who had taken the Seattle training, called it "a great opportunity to learn ways of improving our organization." Much help for mounting this event came from CCEC Credit Union and the Co-op College of Canada.

Work in the warehouse was demanding. At first it seemed that my puny muscles could not be coaxed into hefting a 50-kilogram sack of black beans from a stack onto a pallet to fill a customer's order. Unloading a truck was also exhausting. This lack of strength and stamina was frustrating, especially because the men seemed to have no problem. Paul, who had suffered a back injury the previous year, could still lift more than I could, and even Gerry—who was smaller than I was—could lift the sacks. It wasn't until years later that I learned from Gerry that it had taken just as great an effort on his part. "You remember they were 50-kilo sacks," he told me. "That's 110 pounds. I didn't weigh 110 pounds then!"

As I became stronger, the effort eased slightly. Gradually I learned that gravity could help in many cases, and I could tip the sack from the pile and let it fall into my arms. In putting cases of cheese on the shelves in the walk-in cooler, I learned that it helped to jump a little—by moving my entire body in an upward motion it was easier to shift the case with less strain on the back. Moving a pallet of goods around the warehouse was easy with our manually operated pallet jack—insert the two forks into the pallet's base, pump it up and push or pull to the required position.

We all learned the value of other warehouse equipment. One useful tool for big projects was the pry bar, a six-foot wooden post with a metal lever on wheels that could be used to move such items as grocery showcases. For me the real breakthrough came much later when we bought a barrel lifter. With this piece of equipment we could purchase 650-pound barrels of honey economically from Peace River at a wholesale price, then siphon it into saleable 30-pound pails in the warehouse. The barrel lifter was on wheels. I learned how to shim the ledge under the barrel, press a clamp into place on the top of the barrel, then jump on a crossbar and use my entire body weight to tilt the huge container. It was a glorious feeling to master the honey behemoth and move it around the warehouse. It was even more satisfying when the trucker who had delivered the barrel stood gaping when he was met by two female workers who took the giant barrels in stride. The lewd joke that he had likely planned to tell to the male warehouse workers died on his lips.

No bean or seed supplier left unturned: cashews, sunflower seeds and cheese were popular items and make a complete protein when combined.

When it came time to hire new workers, we took democracy to absurd lengths by insisting on having us all gather in the room, facing the candidate, much like a firing squad. It was a nightmare for the prospective job-seeker and not so much fun for us either. Usually this would happen on a Friday afternoon, the time for our regular weekly meeting when other business needed to be discussed. I recall one poor woman who arrived brimming with confidence and good humour, but after being peppered with questions from all sides, she left shaken and humbled. I do believe we invited her back for a second interview, although my memory could be faulty. She was not hired.

I don't remember precisely when Fred Weihs joined the Brokerage Collective, but we were expanding as a group at this time and had already moved to the larger Burnaby warehouse. He recalls that he stopped by the warehouse on the off chance that there might be employment, and he spoke with Paul and me. We must have been convincing, because he later underwent the firing squad interview.

Fred's degree was in economics, and it was his belief in co-op principles that brought him to our door. His interest in how communities or groups manage their economic life had begun years earlier when he lived on a farm in Quebec over two summers in order to learn French. As the "kid from upper Canada," he had learned that music—the button accordion—was the heart of social interaction in that part of the world and that co-operation with neighbouring farmers was crucial.

Fred was of firm, stocky build with a neatly trimmed beard. With his pleasant good-morning salutations and his desire to open doors for ladies, he was infinitely more polite in his interactions than most of the laid-back characters who came for job interviews. For the first few days after he was hired, he continued to dress in a dapper fashion unsuitable for warehouse work, and he was seen manipulating the pallet jack with a bemused expression that seemed to say: *Is this why I have a degree—to move beans around a warehouse?*

"I learned to wrap cheese," Fred said years later, "and what organic brown rice looked like. I'd never seen it before." He considered the main focus of CRS to be political, though he recognized that it was also social. "Yet it had this imperative that was new for the times."

Paul's recollection is that Fred was not the hippie the rest of us were. "He was straight, as we called it then," Paul said. "I was dubious about that at first until I saw that he was so smart." Fred's intelligence and gift for connecting with people soon shone through.

When we moved into our new warehouse in Burnaby, we had a warehouse-warming party and invited the Fed Up workers. By now we had eased into a workable relationship with them but not before attending many meetings fraught with debate over conflicting ideals. Originally Fed Up was run entirely by volunteers, who were sent by the co-ops to work in the warehouse on a rotating basis. When that proved unwieldy, the trio of staff—the Paid Collective—was formed, and they continued to ask the Brokerage Collective annoying questions, such as, what are you doing? And, why do we need you?

In one issue of Fed Up's newspaper they had listed the Brokerage Collective as a supplier. Nothing wrong with this—we supplied them with beans and cheese—but in this case, they had tucked in a new listing to the effect that we also supplied CANDU nuclear reactors. These were supposedly available in four to forty megatons and cost two billion box tops plus tax. It was a joke, and we laughed, but it was also typical of Fed Up's attitude.

Although the Brokerage Collective met regularly with the staff at Fed Up, nothing grew out of our meetings but frustration. We spent much time dealing with abstracts: ideals, visions and fantasies. In a summary that was likely intended to be sent to the collective, I wrote: "Meetings are marred by dogged persistence over some point of trivia, impetuosity to hasten attack/counterattack strategies, self-conscious avoidance of liberalism: 'I will speak my mind, even if it's late, off the topic, or was obviously not related to what the other person was trying to say.'" Despite this criticism on my part, I have no recollection of what we actually discussed or what these supposed attacks were all about.

Paul had been the person most interested in this exchange of ideas with Fed Up, but even he called a halt to the meetings after a while, stating: "My feeling about this is that I always hoped by agreeing on the ideal we could develop the discussion to a unified position on how to implement the ideal. I realize now that even this was idealistic!" His lofty words were tempered somewhat by the admission that he was lying flat on his back at the time of writing, with a ruptured disc and under the influence of valium.

An underlying issue in these feuds was that of commitment—and it was something CRS would bump into again and again. Two of Fed Up's Paid Collective members told us how committed they were to the cause, how they wanted to work together with us and how our two groups could do work exchanges to understand each other better—but then they left town to live on the land. We took the high ground—they were cop-outs.

But that same year the scene was repeated within our own membership. Two of the group told us they did not want to commit their entire lives to the co-op movement. They did not want to live in the same house as the other members and have to think about and work in the co-op every single day, forsaking other interests. They would resign first. But after a meeting in which commitment was an agenda topic, they decided to stay.

In looking back on these events with the supposed wisdom of years, I understand that they were right. Although I did not actually live with my fellow CRS members in the early years, I lived close by and visited frequently, preferably at dinnertime. I had no TV, no stereo, no car, no pets, no children and no boyfriends who were not involved in co-ops. My social life was intertwined with those of my collective. We went out to events together and celebrated holidays together. At Thanksgiving we lined up two fold-up dining room tables in the living room so that we could seat about twenty people, then cooked up turkey and tofu with veggies and invited guests to bring potluck dishes. On occasion, we gathered at a round table in a Chinese restaurant for lemon chicken and Buddha's feast, or we waited in line at a hole-in-the-wall fish place, The Only on Hastings Street, one of Ros and Dana's favourite restaurants, to sip clam nectar and tuck in to fish and chips.

Meanwhile, our co-op was not growing in a vacuum. Vancouver was a hotbed of societal change in the late 1970s, and all around us were worthy causes and crusades. Marches and protests, speeches and rallies filled our calendars. In 1971 Vancouver Mayor Tom Campbell tried to drive out the many people who had flocked to the West Coast for peace and love by instigating an anti-hippie police rampage in Gastown.

"If these young people do get their way," Mayor Campbell said on the TV news, "they will destroy Canada." In fact, the riots served to bring people together in reaction to the mayor's tactics, and many helping services were born at that time, such as drop-in clinics and temporary hostels.

CRS members took part in community events, going to hear guest speakers at Britannia Centre off Commercial Drive or attending film nights. *Burn!*, a 1969 Pontecorvo film starring Marlon Brando, was a favourite. In the film, set in the nineteenth century, Brando's character is sent to the sugar-cane island of Queimada in the Caribbean to foment revolution, purely in the interest of putting the control of the sugar supply into the hands of one country's merchants. When an indigenous uprising takes place, a leader, José Dolores, emerges, and it is his character that provides the movie's audiences with memorable and inspiring quotes.

"If a man works for another, even if he's called a worker, he remains a slave," says Dolores. "There are those who own the plantation and those who own the machetes to cut cane for the owners." We noted with satisfaction that CRS owned both the plantation and the machetes.

In another scene José Dolores tells one of his rebel soldiers, "If a man gives you freedom, it is not freedom. Freedom is something you alone must take. Do you understand?" When his comrade-in-arms looks confused, José continues: "Well, you will one day, because you've already started to think about it." And that was a crucial statement for our group too. We had already started to think about the changes we were making, and even if we didn't understand the process, we would continue on the path. There was no looking back.

Along with seeking inspiration in books and movies, we shopped and exchanged ideas with members at our own food co-op stores. We joined the annual peace marches calling for nuclear disarmament that had begun in the 1970s as an outgrowth of the anti-war movement. We continued to attend them as the numbers grew into the 1980s, culminating in the 1986 rally when a hundred thousand people marched across Vancouver's Burrard Bridge, calling for an end to the arms race. We went to trade-union rallies in support of strikes and lockouts, while some of us canvassed for the New Democratic Party at election time. Our work was always the prime subject of discussion when we met and made connections with other groups in the community.

The People's Co-op Bookstore on Commercial Drive had been in business since 1945 and was known for its selection of communist and socialist titles. Although we didn't have much involvement with them as a co-op, we were generally sympathetic with their left-leaning direction. When we browsed the store we found many interesting non-fiction works, literature, novels and children's books. It was a place where Jane Austen rubbed shoulders with Karl Marx's *Capital*.

We were not communists—we loathed doctrinaire agendas. Human rights were key: not just in Cambodia, where the ruthless Khmer Rouge leader Pol Pot had taken power, but in our own country among impoverished Native reserves, where children were still being forcibly sent to residential schools. In 1976, after the Museum of Anthropology was opened on the grounds of the University of British Columbia to exhibit First Nations artifacts, Paul and I visited the new building and had our first true glimpse at the art and culture of those who had lived in BC long before European settlers.

In the USA, African Americans were demanding their electoral and other rights. The right to a democratic election had been violated in Chile in the military coup of Augusto Pinochet, which was later to have a profound effect on our co-op.

In Vancouver, activists fought for prisoners' rights, nuclear-free rights and, most importantly to me, women's rights. This included the right of women to choose an abortion, the right to be paid an equal salary for work of equal value and the right to speak up about sexual harassment in the workplace. This was groundbreaking when you consider that prior to that time, wives were considered chattels of their husbands, and it was impossible for a woman to acquire a credit card or take out a loan unless a man signed for it. A woman did not advance to managerial positions in business unless she put up a good fight, earning her such epithets as "ball-buster," "bra-burning harpy" or worse. We CRS members, men and women, denounced the label "chick" from our vocabulary. Chicks were baby hens; women were women.

A Women's Health Collective was set up in Vancouver and staffed mostly by volunteers and some sympathetic doctors. My friend Jenna worked some shifts there and kept me posted as to its progress in helping women take charge of their own health. Transition houses and shelters opened to take in abused women. The Vancouver Status of Women initiated forums and supplied advocates for women in need. They also published a women's newspaper, *Kinesis*, for which I would write during the 1980s. Consciousness-raising groups were springing up. I joined one with a political bent in which a group of women discussed how the class struggle had kept us oppressed—though I'm not sure we found any answers, and the group did not last long.

The many modest co-op businesses that were founded in the 1970s tried to support each other in our activities. Press Gang was a women-owned and managed print shop and publishing business in Vancouver that was founded in 1974. Although it was not legally a co-operative, the women practised co-op principles and were accepted in the community as a co-op. A magazine, *Makara*, started in 1975 and was managed by a collective of women, the Pacific Women's Graphic Arts Co-operative. In one issue of *Makara* they describe their reasons for working as a collective: "We feel everyone should have an equal hand in business decisions and aesthetic judgments, magazine production, equipment-buying, window-washing, etc. It has to do with eliminating hierarchies in as many areas of our lives as possible. It also allows us to learn new skills as we become ready; everyone here is a teacher and everyone is a learner." The magazine was printed at Press Gang Publishers.

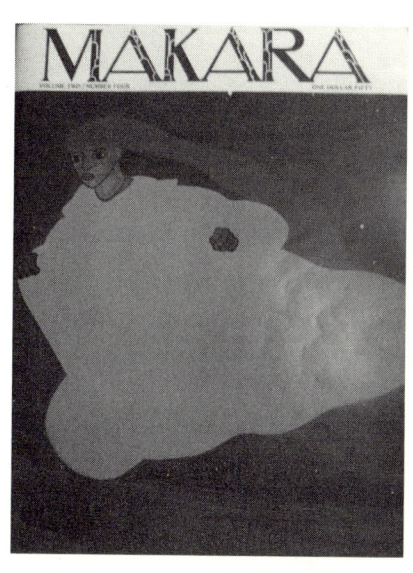

Makara magazine was managed by women who sought to eliminate hierarchies and learn skills.

One day in 1981 I stopped by the Press Gang shop to pick up brochures for the Community Business Training courses that I was organizing. I watched a sad scenario: a lone woman sitting awkwardly at an ancient stapling machine that broke down repeatedly, requiring her to stand up each time and re-thread it. I was no stranger to work that was drudgery, but I felt that this was a sorry example of defective equipment that would not be replaced for lack of funds. Also, the numbing, isolating tasks would not attract new members to the collective. What was the point of continuing in a failing business? I said as much to Lara, who worked with CC Grains, a co-operative food wholesaler in Seattle. I questioned our own involvement in co-ops and our ability as women to operate our own businesses if all we could manage was to eke out a marginal existence, inspiring no one.

"But what are their goals?" she asked. "They may not become a viable worker-managed business as we define it, in terms of sales and profitability, but they may still achieve their goals." It was a shock to consider that this wisdom was true: many of Press Gang's goals were not economic—like *Makara*, they hoped to employ women and train them in non-traditional skills, and they also wanted to be the community's printing press, part of a network. CRS Workers' Co-op hoped to be a viable business serving as the co-op movement's food provider, but we were always reaching for the stars—we wanted to learn new skills as well and to employ women who would share with men in managerial decisions.

THE ACTIVE YEARS—THE 1970S

1972

–De Cosmos Village (East Forty-Ninth and Boundary) is the first housing co-op built as a major development. It was preceded by a "scatter" housing co-op in 1970 called Waterfront Consumer's Co-operative.

–Rosemary Brown is the first black woman to be elected to the provincial legislature.

1973

–The Vancouver Women's Bookstore opens in downtown Vancouver and operates as an oasis for feminist readings, workshops and meetings.

1974

–SPEC recycling has its last day before being taken over by the City of Vancouver.

SPEC, or the Society Promoting Environmental Conservation, is one of the oldest environmental organizations in Canada, promoting recycling and bringing environmental concerns to the public and to policy-makers. SPEC was founded in 1969 in Coquitlam, BC.

–Pauline Jewett becomes president of Simon Fraser University, the first woman to preside over a major Canadian university.

1975

–The first Greenpeace anti-whaling campaign is mounted.

On June 27, 1975, members of Greenpeace Canada took the first ever direct action against whalers who were actively whaling west of California. The Greenpeace activists navigated small inflatable Zodiac boats between the Russian whalers of the *Dalniy Vostok* fleet and the hunted whales. The activists were unable to stop the Russian whalers, but the airing of this event on television was significant in raising public awareness.

–The newly formed, listener-supported Vancouver Co-operative Radio, CFRO 102.7 FM hits the airwaves.

The Co-Op Radio goal was to make radio more accessible to local musicians, minorities and community groups. Volunteer programmers, members of the co-op, put together shows, and listeners paid to become members, providing a source of income for the always under-financed station. It operated out of a previously abandoned heritage building with marble bathrooms and a graceful, winding staircase at Pigeon Park (Carrall and East Hastings). It originally transmitted from Burnaby Mountain and featured a variety of programming, from politics to blues music, and Chinese community shows to lesbian issues. By 1979 it could be heard on cable throughout the province, and in 1982 the transmitter was moved to a more powerful vantage point on Mount Seymour.

Vancouver Co-operative Radio was run by volunteers who delivered eclectic programming.

1976

–Habitat Forum—a counterculture response to the United Nations Habitat Conference on Human Settlements—opens at Jericho Beach.

Habitat Forum and the UN conference took place in Vancouver from May 31 to June 11, 1976. The UN event was billed as a global meeting to discuss human settlements and the contemporary challenges: urbanization, inequality, rural migration to the cities, urban problems, clean water and sanitation. The conference was advised by one of the founders of the field of sustainable development, the economist Barbara Ward, and it was attended by Margaret Mead, Mother Teresa, Buckminster Fuller, Paolo Soleri, Margaret and Pierre Trudeau and many others, and also by key housing and slum activists from around the world.

Habitat Forum was a parallel conference to the UN conference, but it became better known to the public than the official conference. Organizer Al Clapp converted five abandoned air force hangars next to Jericho Beach into a conference site. Hangar 3 was decorated with a huge Haida mural. The Habitat Forum was also memorable for having constructed the world's longest bar. An estimated fifteen thousand people came to the site each day over the two weeks. It also attracted one of our inspirations, Frances Moore Lappé, author of *Diet for a Small Planet*. When Frances came to Vancouver to speak at the conference, someone in CRS invited her to dinner, offering to tell her about our work. She accepted. In our shabby century-old home on Franklin Street, the tables were pulled out to seat a few diners with the renowned personage herself. It's a sure bet that she was served complementary proteins using one of her own recipes.

–Protests continue on behalf of freeing Leonard Pelletier, an aboriginal jailed for allegedly killing FBI agents.

1977

–The new SeaBus ferries begin operating between the Waterfront Station in downtown Vancouver and Lonsdale Quay in North Vancouver.

1978

–The first Vancouver Folk Festival takes place in Stanley Park, starring Bruce Cockburn, Stan Rogers and Roosevelt Sykes.

–Jon Bartlett and Rika Ruebsaat also perform at the first Vancouver Folk Festival.

Singers of traditional Canadian (especially BC) folk songs, the duo continues to collect and publish folklore, and they conduct educational work in schools and run folk song societies and folk music radio shows. Their songs are about real people and real life—traditional ballads and songs from the Industrial Revolution, Canadian lumber camps and American mining towns, shanties and modern political songs. CRS Workers' Co-op member Paul Newman often played bass with them on recordings and at stage performances.

–Pied Pear (Rick Scott and Joe Mock) also appears at the first Vancouver Folk Fest.

Members of this Vancouver-based group (originally known as Pied Pumkin with Shari Ulrich) are still making music into this century.

–An eight-month-long newspaper strike carries on at Pacific Press.

1979

–Granville Island Public Market opens. Prior to that a market had been held on Alexander Street in Gastown occasionally, and the CRS Workers' Co-op had sold Tunnel Canary goods and thirty-pound pails of honey there.

–Doug and the Slugs play the Legion on Commercial Drive.

Chapter 9

TRAVELS AND TEARDOWNS

Paul Newman and I became close as good friends and colleagues, and after his prolonged hospital stay for a back problem, he badly wanted a vacation. We decided to travel together and stay with my friends in Ontario. We boarded a CN train in Vancouver in the dark of winter and planned at which stops we would disembark to see the country. Paul had emigrated from California and wanted to see snow and learn the joys of Canadian cold weather. He succeeded.

Our first stop was in Saskatoon at an early hour in the morning. We were so tired from a sleepless night sitting up on coach seats that we walked to the public library and fell asleep in the comfy chairs. We stayed that night with—who else but some contacts made through the co-op network—and we learned a little more about the issues facing their student co-op.

When we boarded the train again, it was to ride for a longer stretch—this time to Winnipeg, where the train stopped for several hours. Before our arrival, three things were uppermost in our minds about this city: There were many Ukrainians living there, it was often called Winterpeg (for good reason), and the coldest spot in the universe was rumoured to be the corner of Portage and Main. We were determined to experience all three in the few hours of stopover that we were allowed in the city. We jumped off the train and searched the station's phone book for someplace that sold perogies. We travelled by bus to the café, a brightly lighted diner that was serving outsize plates of the butter-fried dumplings stuffed with bacon and potato. We returned to the train by bus, passing the renowned cold corner, and we crossed a bridge that spanned the frozen Red River.

Paul was thrilled and insisted on getting off the bus to view the buildup of ice more closely. I stood shivering in the bitter cold, scarf pulled tight around my face, gloved hands tucked in my pockets while the wind whistled around us and Paul gazed peacefully at the arctic phenomenon. I was happy he was thrilled, but having experienced winter in Ontario, I wanted only to be warm again.

We travelled on to Toronto, where Keith Wallace, my former cheese-researching colleague, picked us up at the station and let us stay at his home. We flew back to Vancouver after Christmas, and immediately on returning, we phoned "home" to the CRS household on Franklin Street.

"We're heading out for dinner at the Indian restaurant on Main Street," said Roger. "Meet us there, and we've got something to show you." I had no doubt that it was a work-related something.

At the corner of Broadway and Main, Paul and I enjoyed a joyful reunion with Dana, Ros and Roger, who swept me up in a big bear hug. We were home; this was my family.

The Indian restaurant, the Himalaya, was popular with the group because it not only served spicy, exotic Indian dishes, but its menu was a chuckle, featuring such delights as "peanuting" chicken, accompanied by Harvey's Tooting Sherry. If asked, the waiter would offer precisely the same description for many of the featured dishes: "It is deep-fried ball." For dessert we chose the rose-scented *gulab jamun*—indeed, a deep-fried ball—or the cardamom exquisiteness of the *ras malai* pudding.

After dinner we walked next door to a closed-up storefront. This unattractive building was what had generated excitement on the part of my colleagues since it contained a wealth of fixtures suitable for a bakery or co-op store: a walk-in cooler, glass display counters, a cash register, aisles of shelves, and many appliances, such as an industrial meat slicer.

"We can get everything in the store for a good price, fixtures and everything, if we knock it down and take it away," Dana informed us with a gleam in his eye. He looked as if he would begin the work at that moment. I envisioned us working until the wee hours, still stuffed with chicken korma, ripping apart shelving and inhaling dust. It was within the realm of possibility.

Ros, as always, was the sensible one. "We can't use all this equipment ourselves," she pointed out. "Let's see if Agora wants to go in with us."

The Agora Food Co-op was in the process of setting up a member-run storefront on Dunbar Avenue, and they had an enthusiastic steering committee with many volunteers to help shift the goods. Yes, they would be interested, several of the members reported.

According to the Main Street building's owners, the deal had to be closed within days since, with the building gutted, they were in a hurry to knock down one wall and rebuild into a three-foot space that had been formerly wasted, thus enlarging the store and upping its value per square foot. It seemed like a lot of work for a few more feet, but their loss was our gain. Within the week, a work party of Agora and CRS volunteers descended on the building to deconstruct it. The day was memorable only because I learned to use a wonder bar, another implement of brilliant design that made me feel strong. I enjoyed wielding tools. With this handy, blue mini-crowbar I could strip door frames, remove nails and stack the structures ready for a convoy of borrowed trucks to take them away. The fact that I was possibly the slowest demolisher in the room didn't bother me. I hummed a tune as I removed one nail to another volunteer's five.

Agora Food Co-op on Dunbar Street opened its doors in 1976 after many months of careful planning. Their steering committee took its role seriously, and because they were launching in an upscale neighbourhood, their products reflected that. I joined this co-op even though I was already a member of the East End Food Co-op at the time because I lived halfway between the two in my attic room in Shaughnessy. As I kept explaining to those who wondered why I chose grocery stores so far away, it was only one bus to Agora and I could carry back a box loaded with the same healthy staples that the other co-ops sold.

In fact there was another reason: it was good to get out from under the shadow of the workers' co-op once in a while. Although Gail had assisted Agora with its set-up, most of Agora's members were removed from other co-op politics. They knew only that they would get good, wholesome food and would chip in their volunteer time in return.

When the time came for Agora to move some heavy equipment that was stored in someone's outbuildings to the new store, I put my name down on the list of moving-day helpers. I noticed that I was the only woman on the list. A friendly fellow phoned me and gently told me that it wasn't necessary for me to help since they would have several strong men to do the dirty work. Miffed, I told him that I worked in a warehouse and was familiar with the operation of moving goods. Oh, and we had a useful pry bar and dollies that they could borrow—though they would have to acquire them through me. To his credit, the fellow lost his condescension immediately and made plans to meet me at our warehouse. I brought the tools out to the loading dock; he thanked me and then reached up to help the lady down the steps. Some habits die hard.

On moving day I realized that I really wasn't up to the task of such physical effort but felt it was important to carry the flag for strong womanhood. I lifted one box to the other men's two and soon found my niche in loading up the dolly so that others could push it to the truck.

When we arrived at the new store, several women were waiting and had volunteered to receive the goods and unpack. One of them looked longingly at the hulking mover men and sighed that she would like to give all the men a good back massage after this strenuous job. It was at that moment that I realized these were not my kind of women—I was much more comfortable with the women of CRS, who no doubt also needed back massages after a day of work in the cannery or the warehouse.

Nonetheless Agora was a friendly co-op, and they hired a manager who many of us at CRS already knew, Will Mitchell. With his straggly beard, ponytail and complete lack of interest in his wardrobe, he was on the edge of some Agora members' comfort zones. However, he won them over with his thoughtfulness and dedication to the store and its principles. Later Will came to work at another co-op project, Uprising Breads Bakery.

Two or three of the CRS workers always attended Fed Up's conferences, which were held in different parts of the province. The first one I ever attended took place in Ootsa Lake, the farthest north that I had ever been. Co-operators from all over the province gathered there to discuss our future as a movement, to talk about items for the catalogue, to meet and connect with one another and to play volleyball outside of the lodge where the meetings were held. Later a few of us took a canoe out on Francois Lake, paddling far out in its calm waters and then stopping to listen to the silence. It was still and peaceful—we could hear each other breathe. So this was what it was like to live in the country, I thought, still a city girl at heart.

In February 1976 the Fed Up Council of Representatives was held in Kitsilano, Vancouver. The agenda listed the usual topics in a curious mixture of formal and informal: regional reports; the Paid Collective report; and newsletter, catalogue and warehouse committee reports. New business was listed as "What Must Be Done." Issues raised included whether to split the work week for some visiting co-ops, allowing them to serve only half a week, and much discussion ensued about recalcitrant co-ops that had not fulfilled their work week commitment. A hot button topic was the "cigarettes and pop decision." Could any item be ordered through Fed Up, even if that item was unhealthy? Why couldn't co-ops order cigarettes or cola in bulk? It was never going to happen, but just as in our workers' co-op, the principle had to be questioned loudly and publicly. The debate was stimulating, if inconclusive. The third part of the meeting was listed as "Separating the Wheat from the Chaff." Surely a good process for any organization!

The following year, 1977, I was very excited to go to Powell River as the CRS representative to Fed Up's Council. When I had first arrived from Ontario, I had thought that I would be happy to take up some job in a small town in BC, maybe 100 Mile House, where a friend of mine had landed, or a coastal town where fishing boats plied the waters and the forests grew down to the sea. It was a romanticized view of the province—as I was soon to find out. After visiting Victoria and comparing it to Toronto, I decided it to be too slow and boring. Powell River would be perfect, I told myself; it was the right size, on the ocean, not too far from Vancouver.

It was winter and dark when I boarded the bus in Vancouver, and I was seated next to another council delegate whose name I now forget. We chatted together on the first ferry, which took me to the Sunshine Coast, and we travelled on winding roads in darkness to the next ferry. There were not many people on the bus by that time; the second ferry seemed very primitive and quiet. It was lonely and dark when we arrived in Powell River to find the conference location in a church hall in what is called the old town. Two other women and I were sent to billet at the home of a bearded, pot-smoking fellow dressed in a colourful cape, who remarked how happy he was to be hosting three lovely chicks. The next day, when I had a good look around at the old town of Powell River—its empty street, the smelly mill pumping out effluent, a trash-laden sidewalk in front of a bar—I decided that Vancouver was really not so bad after all. I wouldn't be moving to the country any time soon.

A later council took many of us, CRS and Fed Up delegates alike, to Nelson by chartered bus, where we gathered along with a contingent of Guatemalan Canada World Youth kids. On Sunday evening, when the conference was coming to a close, the bus driver decided that he would be driving back to Vancouver that night, and he urged the still-voting delegates onto the bus. Gail was concerned that the driver would fall asleep on the way, so she organized a wake-up team of passengers who would take turns making conversation with him. We arrived safely back at the Fed Up warehouse at 6 a.m.

On another occasion we travelled to Osoyoos, where the organic farmers from Cawston and the folks from Princeton gathered to feed and connect with us. It was a further valuable education into the geography and people of the province.

I wasn't going to leave the city any time soon, I had decided, but I was probably in the minority. Many people my age were heading back to the land—forming communal living situations or intentional communities in the fertile valleys of the Kootenays, on Vancouver Island or up north. Alex Berland's history of the Kootenay Co-op, which celebrated its fortieth anniversary in 2015, is in Appendix I.

Chapter 10

FOOD, GLORIOUS FOOD

One day in 1976 the Brokerage Collective received a phone call from one of the staff at a development education group that worked with non-profits in Canada and in the Third World. He wanted to tell us about a co-operative in Tanzania on the east coast of Africa. "They're producing coffee," he said, "and they're looking for markets. You could be the first to bring it to Canada."

We were excited, since we had long wanted to add coffee to our catalogue. The previous year we had received an airmail letter from the exotic land of Papua New Guinea. It was from a Canadian University Service Overseas (CUSO) worker, Haru Bekker-Kanemitsu, who was living and working in that country and who sometimes wrote for the Fed Up newspaper.

"Being temporarily in a Third World country has made me think more about where the food we eat in BC comes from," she wrote in the newspaper. "Through Fed Up we buy high protein foods from other countries...As Frances Moore Lappé points out in *Diet for a Small Planet*, should we be buying protein from countries which need it?" She went on to say that in PNG much of the coffee is grown in small holdings and sold to large factories, and much of the good land is in tea and coffee, removing it from agricultural land that could grow food for its people. Although Haru offered to start the process of buying coffee beans for the Brokerage Collective, we balked at the idea at the time, grasping the wisdom of her comments.

But time passed and we researched this favourite substance, learning that it was the second-largest trading commodity in the world, after oil. Of course Nestlé and other corporations had the upper hand in the market, and it engaged us to think that we would be bringing in coffee under the nose of the marketing giant—and from a co-op yet. At that time Nestlé was not in good odour with the politically active because of their practice of teaching Third World women to give up breastfeeding and buy their formula instead. Though the formula may have been just fine for infants, it had to be mixed with water, and in many developing countries clean drinking water was not available. The babies sickened easily without the benefit of their mothers' milk. Nestlé had become the subject of a widely advertised boycott.

Our initial enthusiasm for the project gave way to some disappointment—it turned out that the coffee was instant and it was made from processed robusta beans, an inferior grade, not the flavourful arabica beans. Robusta coffee beans, we learned, are hardier and more easily grown, as they are less susceptible to insects since they contain more caffeine than arabica beans. This extra caffeine gives robusta a bitter taste, both for the bugs and for the consumer. The cheaper robusta is used in instant coffee or added to a blend of beans to cut costs. Most coffee retailers promoted their 100 percent arabica, the sweeter, tastier bean.

After much wrangling at CRS meetings of the whole, we decided to go ahead anyway. After all, we were supporting a co-operative that was new, and we were making use out of what might have become an underutilized product. Our goods would be fairly traded—not a concept that was much in evidence at the time, but later entire stores and markets would be founded on the idea that First World buyers should pay at a fair rate for goods crafted in Third World countries.

The next hurdle was lengthy: to arrange for money to change hands and for the goods to be shipped at an economical price. CRS did all of its banking through the Gulf and Fraser Fishermen's Credit Union, who told us that they could not help us with the appropriate letters of credit for an international transaction. They were supportive—but were not set up to do it. We had to find a bank that did that sort of thing.

The nearest international banking institution was on the corner of Hastings and Main, in the heart of the downtown eastside. I doubt whether they saw much business in Africa, as their international department was heavily focussed on Asia. However, they were polite, requiring guarantees that we were able to provide. Our names, Jan DeGrass and Paul Newman, were on the line, although we were backed by the workers' co-op and ultimately by the federal government grant.

As we trundled through all the appropriate paperwork for this financial transaction, involving thousands of dollars, I thought about my parents and what they would make of my work. They were ambivalent about my career with the co-ops, their anxieties spilling over the long-distance phone lines in lengthy lectures. My father was convinced that I was only working temporarily until I found a real job, and my mother wondered why on earth I wanted to dress in plaid shirts and steel-toed boots. "Teach your parents well" were the words to a popular song by Crosby, Stills, Nash & Young—"their children's hell will surely go by." It was difficult to convince my parents that I was doing what I considered to be socially responsible work—and the only thing that reassured them was that I was indeed making a living.

When the letters of credit were set up and sent to the supplier, we had to arrange for shipping by freighter. That also required a form to be filled in, which I did with ease, but after sending it, I panicked that it would be misunderstood. By that time we had moved to a warehouse in Burnaby and our address declared that we were no longer in Vancouver, where the port of entry would be. Would they wonder where Burnaby was? Would they know that they should use the port of Vancouver? We sent off a telegram, as I recall, making sure that the co-op knew where to send the goods. It was overkill, but by that time we were paying attention to details. Nothing could go wrong.

Amazingly, nothing did. Months later we received a shipment of instant coffee labelled Africafe, which we promoted to the co-ops. Suddenly everyone in our group was drinking instant and telling each other that we liked it. It tasted fine, but it was not a hit with our markets. I can't remember if we made a second order, but we told the co-op to please get back to us when they were exporting coffee beans. Nestlé could rest easy, as we turned our attention to other goods.

Markets were finding us. We did little advertising and relied on personal contact through phone calls and mailing lists. This non-system that allowed markets to contact us was proving paradoxical. Since businesses were more aggressive than co-ops in locating new suppliers, we quickly added many new businesses, such as health food stores, to our markets, which was good for revenue but also disappointing, as it tended to define the products we handled. Our original goal was to serve the co-ops. We wanted to be more in touch with co-op needs and to feel we were supplying a worthy service.

By 1977 the Brokerage Collective had added almonds, cashews and more beans, this time from the Ontario Bean Growers co-op: our original product, black turtle beans, plus red kidneys, navy beans, light kidneys, white kidneys and yellow-eye beans. We proudly wrote in the Fed Up newspaper that by spring we would be carrying nearly every variety of bean grown in Canada. We also reported that though sales had been good, our markup was low, and that currently any funds left after paying overhead and loan payments went into stocking new items. We ended our cheerful list with the following epilogue: "So, folks, don't forget that beans and cheese have complementary proteins, that honey is really just bee poop, and if black turtles are slow, at least they keep you steady." It was signed Paul, Jan, Gerry and a fellow who worked with us for a short time, Phil Vernon.

By 1977, the CRS food wholesaler catalogue had grown to include a huge variety of goods, everything from sunflower oil to tofu and walnuts shipped from China.

The CRS truck, seen here on Commercial Drive, was kept busy transporting goods to and from the bakery and making deliveries to Fed Up for its member co-ops.

In 1978 I drafted a more complete official catalogue of our goods. It extolled the virtues of the co-operative way, listed the products for sale from the wholesaler and the cannery, and went on way too long over how to control grain moths in the nuts and seeds—a section that probably lost us some customers. It was not my best promotional effort.

The next few catalogues were much bushier. Seeds such as sesame and sunflower had been added to the list, along with lentils and flax. We added pasta of various types, including soy shells and whole-wheat spaghetti obtained from our Seattle co-op wholesaler friends, along with organically grown stone-ground flours and expeller-pressed oils from safflower, sesame, olive and sunflower. Nuts and raisins proved to be a big seller, and we learned a lot about them. Many of the product lines were as new to us as they were to our customers. Would bread rise enough using stone-ground flour? What did cold-pressed oil mean? In the days before Google, we raided the library for information about our food. When Paul discovered a picture of cashew nuts growing on a tree, the curvaceous nut budding from a plant the size of a golf ball,

Liz Weis unloads the distinctive yellow CRS delivery truck.

we were in awe. Having never travelled to a tropical place, we couldn't imagine such things.

Sometimes a case would arrive broken, its contents spilling out, and these we declared available to the collective for lunches. Fred proved ingenious in combining several disparate ingredients to make a warehouse lunch: egg noodles with giant, sugary lexia raisins tossed together with a can of soup and covered with cheese. Though we did not sell alcohol, I considered it my task to design a suitable drink for after-work soirees. My beverage combined an organic apple/apricot juice, honey, ice and vodka. I called it Summer Warehouse.

Chapter 11

GIVE US BREAD BUT GIVE US ROSES

The CRS Workers' Co-op's official incorporation papers were signed on June 9, 1976, during the third and last year of CRS's grant funding. I remember signing the charter document in the living room of the house, since demolished, on the corner of Woodland and First Avenue, which was every bit as noisy with traffic as that area is now.

When CRS had begun, before my time, the initials had stood for Consumer Resource Services. There's no indication in any of the many reports sent to government officials as to why this confusing moniker. It was a misleading name. The public was forever phoning us in the mistaken notion that they were calling some kind of a better business bureau, and they wanted to complain about the service from their washing machine repairman or to cancel their magazine subscriptions. In 1976 the co-op was officially renamed the Collective Resource and Services Workers' Co-operative.

Incorporated under the Co-operative Associations Act, CRS listed seven goals on its mission statement. The first was to establish or include, as part of the association's activities, businesses or industries that were to be operated and wholly controlled by the members who worked in them. Other provisions encouraged collective ownership and allowed the sale of one-hundred-dollar shares to each member. Operating costs would be met through revenue generated by the sale of goods and services, with consumer co-operatives—that is, the food co-ops—being the priority market. The last item on the statement of intent read that, "Women and men who work together as members of this association will do so on the basis of strictest equality." It was an important ethic, especially during the 1970s when women were surrounded by so-called male chauvinist pigs, and it was this egalitarian principle that kept many women involved in the co-op movement. But policing "strictest equality" was practically impossible. Dana wrote up the statement of intent after major input during endless meetings of the whole, but he struggled with that last sentence. He brought a draft to the meeting that read: "Will end this sentence in a way that does not sound pretentious."

The first signature on the incorporation papers was that of Gail Cryer, who listed her occupation as organizer. The others, including me, signed on the next page. Sheila Adams listed her occupation as canner, as did Rosalind Breckner and Roger Inman. Dana Weber and Cam Ford listed their occupations as baker. Gerda Osteneck worked at Queenright and called her occupation "woodworking shop worker." Paul Newman and I signed as "wholesaler workers." Though others were involved at the time of signing, they are not all listed, because the Co-op Act required only five people to form a co-operative.

The official memorandum of association allowed the group to own and operate food-processing plants, workshops, yards, warehouses, farms and bakeries. A few of the CRS members, especially Dana, had been making plans throughout 1976 to start up a bakery. Thus Uprising Breads Bakery, one of CRS's great successes, opened its doors just before Christmas in 1976. LEAP funding had dried up by that December just two weeks before the bakery opened, and we were required to either work in the businesses we had built, paying ourselves salaries, or find other employment. Several of us went on unemployment insurance (as it was called then) while we sought other jobs, though we continued to volunteer in our various industries, including the set-up of the new bakery.

The handwritten notes in the minutes book that was started at the beginning of 1977 reflected a wave of anxiety about how we would continue to pay ourselves. Our final LEAP payment, due in October 1976, had not arrived by January 1977, and our accountant, Dick McGinnis, began checking the feasibility of paying wages from our industries. There were murmurings from some members about dipping into a Fund Centrale, as it was called, in which money from the various income sources would be pooled. In typical meeting procedure we went around the room requesting that each person state how much they needed to live on, and these would be our financial goals. Most required at least three hundred dollars per month, and in the case of those with dependents—an older man was the only one in that category—they would require four hundred dollars per month plus one hundred dollars for each child. Gerry noted that three hundred dollars would feel like welfare and recommended determining expenses first. The minutes record that I asked for three hundred dollars plus medical benefits. Some said that they could live on as little as one hundred dollars per month with the promise of an increase in the future. Looking back, these years—our twenties—should have been our money-earning years. They were not.

As we expanded, all the groups needed new staff. The Brokerage Collective had recently acquired Fred but had a need for part-time help in the warehouse, so Gail began to divide her time between the bakery and the brokerage. Ron Hansen had joined the co-op, and he worked with Dana and Gail to build the bakery. As the oldest member of the group, then in his forties, Ron was often the voice of reason at our meetings—he would methodically explore our choices and offer his firm opinion. I recall that he was famous for a unique form of decision making. We could choose x or y or Ron's third alternative: we could do nothing. Often that third choice was the most sensible path.

Our political consciousness was raised by the hiring of Chilean refugees—or, for a better description, escapees. Nestor Fernandez was the first. He arrived at the Burnaby warehouse for a Friday evening job interview with the firing squad of all the CRS workers, and he told us a little of his story in his accented English. When the Pinochet regime began its reign of terror, he had fled the country, arriving in Canada shortly before his interview. He believed strongly in the principles of the previous Marxist-leaning government that, we learned, had been democratically elected.

During the course of our usual rapid-fire questions, Wendy, one of our newest staff members, asked him if he had ever been in jail. The room went silent. Nestor, visibly sweating, squirmed in his chair. No one helped him out—we all waited for his answer. Finally he admitted that yes, he had been thrown in jail, but he wanted us to know that this was not uncommon during the military rule that he had experienced. "In my country anyone can be put in jail," he said, "for doing something ordinary."

He was not a criminal. Wendy apologized for putting him on the spot, and Nestor was hired unanimously. At that time we did not comprehend the forces that had impelled Nestor and other Chileans to flee their country, but little by little we heard more stories.

Our next Chilean candidate, Nelson Rodriguez, was a large man in his forties with a family who had come with him to Canada. He had not been politically active; in fact, he had done his best to keep out of the way of political opposition, but one day when a workers' protest had been called, he had stayed home from work. For this he was fired and jailed.

> In 1973 the left-leaning, democratically elected president, Salvador Allende, appointed Augusto Pinochet as commander-in-chief of the Chilean Army. In September 1973 Pinochet led a military coup against Allende's government, starting an authoritarian military dictatorship that employed terror and torture against all citizens suspected of adhering to leftist politics.
>
> It was later estimated that during the Pinochet regime (1973 to 1990), approximately 35,000 people were victims of human rights abuses, with 28,000 tortured, 2,279 executed and 1,248 "disappeared." [Ref. National Commission on Political Imprisonment and Torture (Valech Report) and the Commission of Truth and Reconciliation (Rettig Report).]
>
> Chilean prisoners and their families and friends endured electric shocks, waterboarding, beatings and sexual abuse. Some disappeared. The tactic of "disappearing" the enemies of the Pinochet regime was systematically carried out during the first four years of military rule.
>
> Canadian diplomats were slow to respond but eventually generated momentum to bring persecuted Chileans to Canada, and ultimately Canada included refugees as a special class in its immigration act.

During the next year, we hired other Chileans: Rosacruz Toledo, who worked in the bakery, and charismatic Carmengloria Quiroz, whose blond, striking good looks sent at least two of the males in our co-op into romantic tailspins. Later Natasha Villasenor was also hired and she worked in the cannery until its eventual demise. A few of the Chileans set about organizing popular festive events called *peñas* at various venues in Vancouver, featuring music, dancing and tasty dishes—including empanadas, the meat pie of Chile, baked on occasion at Uprising Breads.

The bakery was located at 1697 Venables, not far from Commercial Drive, and it occupied the corner storefront plus another large room behind. The building had been built in 1910 and had been re-floored using several layers of plywood. Dana remembers discovering this when the trio of Dana, Gail and Ron Hansen poured a huge concrete pad as a base for the oven in the front retail space of the building.

Our giant oven had sat in pieces for over a year by 1976, and members of CRS were weary of moving the pieces to different storage areas. Dana recalls that finally a friend in Strathcona who had been storing it in his shed wanted it out of the way, so when Gail discovered a suitable building for rent on Venables, CRS was happy to sign a lease and move the oven to its new home. It was up to Ron Hansen to puzzle over how to fit the various pieces of the oven together, but eventually he solved this challenging problem.

The oven's provenance was unclear to us at the time, but in later years Ron Pither related the true story behind it. Details are sketchy but it seems that a group of social activists in the United States, including folk singer Joan Baez, had been seeking a tax exemption so that their taxes would not go to financing the war in Vietnam. Instead, they sought other more worthy purchases—money for ploughshares, not for swords. They made a phone call to a Canadian acquaintance to inquire about a granola-making collective in Fort Langley whose product they had enjoyed in California. The granola workers were about to disband and sell or give away their oven if only they could find someone who would put it to good use. Ron Pither happened to be present at the time of the phone call, and this hot tip was enough to make Ron and a friend jump

The Uprising Breads Bakery: the doorway to tantalizing aromas, sweet pastries and wholesome bread.

Uprising Breads has been at the same location since 1976, at the corner of Venables Street and Commercial Drive in Vancouver.

in a truck and drive to the granola bakery to take the oven themselves. "We 'claimed' it," Ron remembers, "as we considered ourselves as having the most political correctness at the time."

In hindsight the retail area was not a great location to place this huge, ugly oven, as it became a focal point for the room in an area that should have been more aesthetic for customers. Also, it warmed up the room considerably. Fortunately, customers were distracted from this eyesore by an old-fashioned glass showcase and counter, before they chose their baked treat and paid for it at the old-fashioned cash register. Was there a single piece of equipment that had not been recycled or reused from another source? I don't think so, unless the refrigerator was new. Possibly. We had also acquired other equipment: a proofer, a noisy bread slicer and a large sheeter/moulder. When the bakers passed the dough through the sheeter rollers, it was flattened and turned on to a canvas belt. A chain picked it up and rolled it into a loaf shape. Fun to operate but like all the equipment, it had a steep learning curve.

Dana came up with the perfect name for the bakery: Uprising Breads. In the shop's interior, everything was painted in yellow and

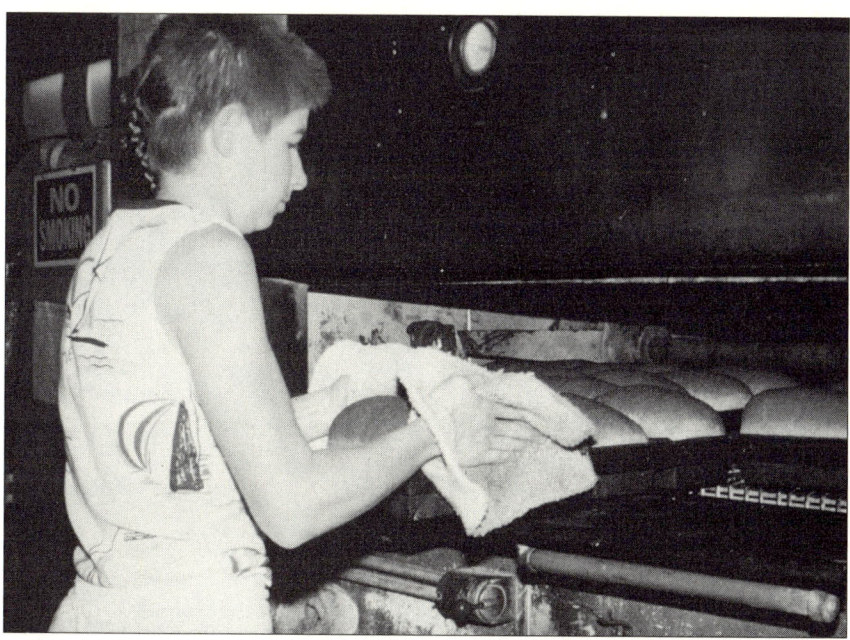

(Above) Janet Cooke removes loaves from the oven. The huge, ugly oven occupied a big chunk of retail space until Uprising Breads was redesigned in the 1980s.

Uprising Breads worker Debbie Hollett checks whether the pastries are browning.

Joan Makaroff added her experience as a professional chef to the Uprising Breads staff.

brown, earthy and funky, to indicate we were not your typical gleaming commercial business that produced white fluff bread for the masses. Our masses were those who sought whole grains, those who were realizing that nutrition was important or who sought alternatives such as our carob/sunflower squares. These used a sweet chip derived from the locust bean pod as a substitute for chocolate. Who needs a substitute for chocolate? It was a sign of how seriously we took our work; we wanted to offer alternatives. Organic grains were to be found only in health food stores in those days, and we tried to incorporate them into the loaves. We were providing a market niche in wholesome foods that were baked carefully by workers conscious of nutrition.

The members/owners of CRS who were not bakers learned how to be bakers. Gail, Ron Hansen and Dana went to Vancouver Vocational Institute to take the night school course, and it was Dana who made the first attempt at sourdough white bread. Gerry recalls: "The loaf looked gorgeous. We let it cool in anticipation and then found that we could

The Finnish whole-grain bread was a big seller; the cinnamon buns were hot from the oven and the raisin scones were light and tasty.

not cut it." Much to Dana's disgust, the residents of Franklin Street hung the loaf on two nails on the kitchen wall, and they used the loaf for a hammer, which came in handy to reinforce the nails holding up the rickety kitchen table.

Gail loved the act of baking, but her first occasion of using the mixer left her ridden with anxiety. "We didn't know what we were doing," Gail said. "We were told, 'Don't let it over-mix, or it won't rise.'" They had no idea what exactly that meant or how to time it. "We were so stressed that first night," she recalls. They made twelve loaves that night and twenty-four the next night—not exactly a high volume of production. As they learned more, they increased their production and took suggestions for new products from the staff. Gail suggested making egg bread challah, braided into three strands. Then at 2 a.m. one night shift, she decided to learn how to braid into six strands, and she called for help from a friend who was a professional baker. Despite the late hour, he hastened to the bakery to show her how it was done.

This was typical of the kind of support that we continued to get from all sides. The flour salesman, Fred Abraham, for example, sat down at the bakery one day on his own time and revised the fruitcake recipe. Other volunteers from Fed Up co-ops stopped by to lend a hand and see what it was like to work in a bakery. Though we didn't have the LEAP grant support of the government for this project, we sure had the support of the neighbourhood.

Many customers also welcomed us. One lovely woman with a plummy British accent stopped in while Gail was up a ladder fixing something, and she noted the wonderful work that "we girls" were doing. In the 1970s, when women were struggling for equality, we appreciated any notice, any praise of how important or how strong we were. We loved that woman—but never found out her name.

The bakery was just down the street from the Vancouver East Cultural Centre or "The Cultch" as everyone called it. Some of the Tamanhous Theatre actors were regular customers for years. Also, the day shift from the nearby marble factory used the bakery for their coffee breaks. I always remember the short, fat guy who we called "raisin scone" since that was his favourite item.

Soon everyone learned how to use the equipment, how to weigh the ingredients in pounds and ounces and how to make the goods appeal to the public. Cam Ford rolled up his sleeves and learned to make pastry. Dana, who had long wanted to bake on a commercial scale, designed recipes and produced winners. His round loaf of Finnish whole-grain remained a bestseller for years. The sourdough pumpernickel was chewy and hearty; the oatmeal raisin bread was delightful and a precursor of our stellar hot cross buns. Personally I liked the cracked wheat and sunflower bread with its nutty taste and seeds that crackled in the toaster.

Joan Makaroff joined the group during the first year of the bakery, and she was the only trained professional chef among us. In her quiet, friendly way she taught others techniques for baking and contributed a popular recipe: oatmeal chocolate chip cookies. Will Mitchell, who had to wear a net over his wispy beard, was a mine of retail information developed during his managerial role at Vancouver's Agora Food Co-op, and he worked the nighttime bread shift for years. Ann Mackay inspired others with her ability to work quickly and efficiently.

Over those first few years, many other members learned how to run the bakery: Debbie Eaton, Nestor Fernandez, Carmengloria Quiroz,

The Uprising Breads Bakery gang in 1987. That's Ron Hansen on the left looking managerial in a suit. Debbie Eaton holds her baby and Isabelle Truscott has also brought her son to work. The tall fellow in back is Roger Inman who worked at the bakery after the cannery's closure.

Rosacruz Toledo, Nelson Rodriguez, Maureen Collier, Barry Maxwell, Wendy Legare, Ken Waldron, Sandy Oliver. Ros and Gerry were the bookkeepers, but they were also required to dip their hands in flour more than once. After the closure of the cannery in 1978, Roger also worked tirelessly on many bakery shifts.

Although Paul, Fred and I constituted the Brokerage Collective (food wholesaler) at that time, we also chipped in—we were doing "production" at the bakery, a valued work ethic. We tested our abilities in speed and quality. We learned a lot. Once a person learns how to flip a tray of hot cinnamon buns just out of the oven in front of the watchful eyes of customers without dropping anything or sticking her hands with syrup, that person has made a friend of bakeries for life. I could write a sidebar on the topic of cinnamon buns alone.

Taped music played in the bakery while the morning shift took bagels out of the freezer and boiled them, ready for baking as our first customers from the neighbouring businesses opened the door to the warmth and yeasty aromas. The ambience was delightful, so much so that Denny Boyd in his *Vancouver Sun* column remarked about his favourite place, Uprising Breads, where he could hear jazzy sounds among the fuzzy-headed bakers.

We decided that a grand opening celebration for the bakery in 1976 might be a red flag to the governmental agencies that were now paying us weekly on our unemployment insurance, and we would be accused of fraud. Therefore, we did not advertise the opening, making it possibly the most low-key launch of all time. We did not decide to pay the first salaries until we realized that some of the bakery's best customers were the government clerks who processed our unemployment claims and, if we recognized them, they were bound to have recognized us.

We finally held our gala celebration the following year, just before Christmas 1977. It was dark outside that December evening, but within the bakery all was light and music. Fred with his button accordion and Paul with his upright bass played a slow waltz tune—"Newfoundland Lament," as I recall. Taking my hands out of the dishwater, I danced around the bakery in my steel-toed boots (boys' size) and my flannel shirt. We always dressed for the occasion.

Dana arrived with the champagne and set to uncorking it, his brow furrowed with concentration, teeth over his lips and burrowing into his shaggy beard. I know this for a fact because someone captured a photo of him. Was the photographer Gerda, who later went on to open a camera store up north? Or was it Gerry? Not sure. For that glorious party we probably put out some trays of sausage rolls, Eccles cakes and blueberry scones. We might have had Christmas stollen for sale, or fruitcake. We served coffee, and I'm sure there was more than one bottle of something stronger being passed around. Everyone danced a little, while some busied themselves preparing for the morning shift—but with smiles on their faces.

Later someone gave me a ride to the airport and, clutching my backpack and a box of cannery jam intended as gifts, I boarded a red-eye flight to spend Christmas with my parents. But when I left my co-op workplace, it felt as if I was leaving home.

Chapter 12

A CHANGE IS GONNA COME

Change had been the key word for the first months of 1977. The LEAP grant funding had ended just two weeks before the bakery opened and at the same time as the Queenright Beekeepers went into voluntary liquidation. Although Queenright had been considered part of the co-op and the collective members were paid by the grant salaries, they had incorporated separately from CRS in their desire to be a producers' co-operative of beekeepers. However, it had been difficult for Queenright to manage both the beekeeping operation in Dawson Creek and the shop production and marketing in Vancouver. Day-to-day decisions had been made by the shop workers in Vancouver, and communication between the two sites was not consistent. In the 1975 season the production of honey had amounted to four thousand pounds, not a huge yield, considering they maintained 109 colonies.

Since the operation of Queenright had been almost completely subsidized by the LEAP grant, which had come to an end, CRS became the creditor and was entitled to take the equipment to offer it for sale, according to an agreement made at Queenright's time of incorporation. This amounted to specialized woodworking equipment for making bee boxes, and enough beekeeping equipment to service a hundred colonies, including brood chamber packages and twenty overwintered colonies.

It was the task of the five Queenright directors—Cam Ford, Phil Laflamme, Gerda Osteneck, Ron Pither and Anne Williams—to wind down the co-op. The monies they had generated over the three years went into CRS's account. At this point total worker donations from all industries amounted to about eighty thousand dollars—providing a solid financial base for both bakery and wholesaler.

In my first year with CRS, I had learned much co-op lore. CRS Workers' Co-op followed the co-operative principles, also known as the Rochdale Principles, named after a group of nineteenth-century weavers in Rochdale, Lancashire, England. Working conditions in the cotton mills and coal mines were abysmal; the labourers lived in crowded two-room row houses and shared one lavatory to each street. Disease, dampness and insects were rife, but worse, there was little hope of breaking out of this life because of the impossibility of surmounting the class barriers that kept the majority of the workers plodding away at their tasks.

In 1844 a group of impoverished weavers established a buying co-operative on Toad Lane (today this location is a museum in their honour) in an attempt to combat exploitation by the big mill companies that employed so many and set prices in their company stores. The workers had no union, and the mill owners were deaf to their pleas for a wage increase. Twenty-eight members (twenty-seven men and one woman), mostly flannel weavers, wool sorters or hatters and shoemakers, signed up to pay two pence a week to operate a shop providing basic necessities: flour, butter, sugar and oatmeal. As the membership grew, a code of co-operative principles also grew that has come to be known as the Rochdale Principles.

After the slow start in 1844, the co-op store grew, and by 1944 it had acquired over thirty-six thousand members in many branch stores. It developed into a phenomenon that flourished throughout Britain into the present-day chain of co-ops in which consumers became members, purchased shares, shopped for better value, and received a dividend from the profits earned at the end of the year. But when the co-ops pursued economic growth and considered that to be a standard for success, they soon resembled the companies that they sought to replace.

Sadly, the growth of co-ops in England did not change the overall conditions for the British worker. By the 1930s, when George Orwell wrote his diatribe, *The Road to Wigan Pier*, set in a similar Lancashire mining town, not much had changed. At CRS, even in our first year of operation, we had already come to realize why: co-ops were tiny islands in a vast sea of capitalism.

Two main Rochdale principles define co-ops. The first one is about the vital key—ownership. A co-op is owned equally by all members through the sale of shares. It is open to all people who accept the responsibilities of membership, without social, political or religious discrimination. This fit perfectly with our sense that we must combat exclusion and racism, since that was the right thing to do—though I often wondered what would happen if a neo-conservative or a flagrant evangelist were to join our group. Would we accept their membership in hopes of changing their views?

The second Rochdale principle is that of democratic decision-making—whether by consensus, delegate vote, board or committee decision. No one could say CRS did not comply with this principle. We held endless meetings to determine each step forward, according to everyone's satisfaction. One member holds only one vote in a co-operative; they will never be able to hold more votes, since that would upset the equal balance of power. Although a hired manager does not have a vote, the members take the manager's report and recommendations into account. In the early years we saw no need to hire a manager, since we were all learning and developing our abilities for running our own industries.

CRS struggled with the third important principle, that of returning surplus to the members. Profit was not called profit—it was called surplus and was a benefit to the collective whole. It must be distributed to each member (as in the dividends given to members of the British co-op stores) or be ploughed back into the business. In our case surplus was always returned to the co-op, which meant no dividend or bonus cheque for us at the end of the year. At the time we didn't understand how that might affect an individual's future savings. We all had low incomes and no one saved for the future—but hey, we were all equal.

It was during this period that I learned much about the history of the co-op movement in Canada. It had been a desire for a fair price for their grain that spurred Canadian farmers to pool their resources. In 1923 the Alberta Wheat Pool and the Saskatchewan Wheat Pool were started by frustrated farmers to market their wheat directly to importers rather than through the grain exchange and futures markets. With the addition of the Manitoba Wheat Pool (1926), these co-operative organizations grew in numbers and political power. By 1928 the combined Alberta, Saskatchewan and Manitoba Wheat Pools were among the biggest business concerns in Canada.

> The six original Rochdale principles were adopted by the International Co-operative Alliance (ICA) in 1966 and have been revised since. In 1995 the ICA adopted a revision that appears here in short form:
>
> **1. Open Membership**: Co-ops are open without exception to anyone who needs their services and freely accepts the obligations of membership.
>
> **2. Democratic Control**: Co-ops are controlled by their members, who together set policy, make decisions and elect leaders who report to them. In primary co-ops each member has one vote.
>
> **3. Economic Participation**: All members contribute fairly to their co-ops, which they own in common. Co-ops pay a limited return (if any) on money people have to invest to become members. Surpluses are held for the future and used to improve the co-op's services.
>
> **4. Independence**: All agreements that co-ops sign with outside organizations or governments should leave the members in control of the co-op.
>
> **5. Co-operative Education**: Co-ops offer training to their members, directors and staff. Co-ops inform the public about what they are and what they do.
>
> **6. Co-operation among Co-operatives**: Co-ops work together through local, national and international structures to serve their members.
>
> **7. Community** (a 1995 addition to the original Rochdale Principles): Co-ops meet members' needs in ways that build lasting communities inside and outside each co-op.

In BC the Fraser Valley Milk Producers Association was formed in 1917 to let dairy farmers own and operate their own business, Dairyland. In Nova Scotia co-operators gathered at St. Francis Xavier College in Antigonish to develop co-operative ideals. The Antigonish Movement (at the Coady Institute of St. Francis Xavier) evolved in the 1920s from the pioneering work of Reverend Dr. Moses Coady and Reverend Jimmy Tompkins. As in Rochdale, England, this local community development movement was a response to the poverty afflicting farmers, fishers, miners and other disadvantaged groups in eastern Canada.

In western Canada the consumer co-op movement was dominated by Federated Co-operatives Limited. Started in 1928, Federated was comprised of locally owned retail co-operatives who worked together to form provincial wholesalers in order to expand their buying power. These co-operative outlets in the four western provinces joined together to form Federated. Their reach was extensive—not only in the retail sector, with stores across BC, mainly in rural or suburban areas, but also with interests in oil refineries, sawmills and the feed and fertilizer business. Federated was a huge operation—and though it was a co-operative, we scorned it because it was too commercial, too old guard. We were the new wave of co-ops, as we had been dubbed in the co-op literature. The name Fed Up for the association of small, pre-order, member-run co-ops was a play on the name Federated but also an announcement that members were fed up with corporate co-ops that we felt had forgotten their original idealistic goals.

There were some exceptions. The Mid-Island Consumer Services Co-operative, better known as the Hub Co-op in Nanaimo, was a powerful proponent of collective endeavours and was also a Federated Co-op. We were interested in the success of the Hub and decided to visit this phenomenon. Gail and I piled into her green Volkswagen Beetle and took the ferry to Nanaimo. At the time, the Hub had close to seven thousand members and was doing $13.4 million a year in sales. A Mid-Island Co-op pamphlet titled *Yes... We Can!*, written for members in 1980, included these powerful words: "I live in a world where most men are divided against one another in a struggle for profits. If I spend my money in a business place operated for profit, I am but a part of a system for building profits for others—a mere servant of the business."

I can't remember exactly what our goals were in visiting the co-op—perhaps to see if we could retain our principles as we grew—but I do remember we were, to use a British term, gobsmacked by the extent of this major retail force. Our food co-ops were small and funky; this co-op was big and professional. We had booked our appointments with the head manager at the time, hoping to meet the president of the board, Hume Compton, whose work with the co-op's direct-charge system had added a new dimension to the co-operative. The two percent surcharge for members on their purchases and a minimal weekly fee allowed the co-op great financial stability. In turn, the store retailed food at as low a cost as possible to benefit the members.

On the day of our visit we met the current manager, whose name I forget but whose education on the matter of shelf space was enlightening. He explained how each product had to pay its way for the amount of shelf space that it took up—or it didn't get on the shelf. This was a huge contrast to Fed Up's approach of having members suggest items for the catalogue and voting on which products to carry.

Gail, who had written the manual on organizing storefront co-ops, was fascinated by this approach to economic stability. We understood it almost instantly, although it was a new concept to us. We sold products because we wanted to, because they were what we thought people needed, or because they used up something that would be wasted. We didn't sell products for their ratio of profit per foot of shelf space.

Likely some of this forward-thinking initiative came from the Hub's president, Rod Glen. He was the leadership of this co-op from its inception to his death in 1980, and he had a keen grasp of co-operative ethic, along with the financial understanding that made it successful. Glen had been born on Vancouver Island in the coal-mining community of Ladysmith. He began a career in newspapers and worked at the *Nanaimo Daily Free Press* and their employees' union for nearly twenty years. Although he was associated with many other organizations, including the Nanaimo Credit Union, he is best remembered for his work in developing countries. In 1966 he was elected president of the worldwide organization of credit unions, CUNA International; he was the first non-American to achieve this honour. The position took him to many parts of the world, notably Africa and South America. To this day, Glen is recalled as being an inspiring influence on many small co-operatives in the Third World, as he helped them join the cash economy and have greater control over their food production. Closer to home we had our own co-op heroes and heroines. Ros, Dana and Paul Phillips are remembered as being instrumental in the set-up of many co-ops in BC in the early 1970s, several of which are still flourishing. Keith Jardine, one of Fed Up's first Paid Collective members, went on to work at co-op development for most of his career.

"Yes...We Can!" says the brochure from Nanaimo's big Hub Co-op. And yes, they could... impress Gail Cryer and me when we visited in 1976.

Chapter 13

BLOWING IN THE WIND

By the end of 1978 and with approximately fifteen staff in the cannery, brokerage and bakery combined, CRS members were finding that they were performing two roles: spending much time in production—either baking, canning or wholesaling—but even more time meeting and making management decisions.

By this time, I had moved into the Franklin Street house and taken an upstairs back bedroom (previously occupied by some annoying mice). It overlooked an autobody shop and beyond that Hastings Street. Since all of the other residents—Paul, Joan and Dana—were also involved in CRS, shop talk continued far into the evening hours. If we had been employed by another business enterprise, we would have considered our work to be going into overtime. In fact, there was no overtime pay, and without the grant funding, we were paying ourselves a minimal wage.

In 1982 Dana wrote a case history report about the period of 1971 to 1981 for CRS, and it was presented to the Coady Institute Consultation on Workers' Co-operatives: "In the tradition of kickbacks, we were now capitalizing ourselves with retained earnings based on minimal salaries. It was clearly an organizational strategy that required from members a great deal of commitment and willingness to sacrifice. Indeed, some people called it self-exploitation."

The issue was how to provide for each member according to his or her individual needs while still ensuring that we were earning equal pay. Each person got the same base salary, but now members who had to support dependents received an additional allowance. It was the beginning of a more practical restructuring process that would see the management divided into four committees: personnel (bringing an end to the firing-squad interviews), planning (which had always been important but accomplished on an informal basis), finance and co-ordination.

Fred's push was always toward seeing CRS operate more in the mainstream. "It was said that we were providing a model of how worker-owned industries could be successful," he noted in a 2016 interview. But if so, he argued, weren't we isolating ourselves by staying so closely aligned with the new wave of co-ops? Shouldn't customers of the giant grocery stores be able to buy the bread made in a bakery owned by a workers' co-op and thus see the model at work?

Fred volunteered to put some of his working hours into determining a new management structure. He had embraced with great enthusiasm the concept of all CRS members working together, and he recalls the early days when he learned such things as how to wrap cheese, the properties of organic brown rice and even how to bake croissants when he filled in on bakery shifts. Management up to that time had been ad hoc—now he felt the group needed something more concrete. He saw that some members tended to dominate the meetings, and it was important to develop a structure that would formalize the new committees and operate with *Robert's Rules of Order* to protect the voices of quieter members.

"A new management structure would give a voice to everyone," he said. "It was a way to guarantee democracy." He presented the draft of the four-committee management structure to the group, and though it was greeted with some resistance, it was adopted in 1979.

Revolutions devour their children, remarked the French writer Pierre Vergniaud during that country's uprising. You will sometimes hear it paraphrased: The left always eat their young. The phrase allows for many interpretations, but in my interpretation it means that left-leaning people are harder on and more critical of themselves than others are of them. That was certainly the case with us.

While I was working at the retail counter at Uprising Breads early one morning, a teenage indigenous man came in to buy a pastry. He dithered at the counter, and because it was early and not that busy, I chatted to him, made a joke about something and I laughed. He may have smiled, but he didn't respond. Mohamed was working with us at the time and he overheard my laughter. When the customer left, Mohamed upbraided me for laughing at, as he termed it, the oppressed Native. I was shocked by the allegation and I felt guilty, as if I had indeed been mocking the man in a politically incorrect way. Mohamed persisted in his criticism and told me that my racist roots were showing.

Looking back, I can see that there was certainly truth to be explored by our mostly all-white and mostly middle-class collective at the time. Mohamed, with his black skin, challenged several of us by asserting his sensitivity to race. My awareness of racial tension was heightened, and in best co-operative fashion, we made it a subject for our meetings and for further consciousness-raising sessions.

We were white bread, said Ron Pither, recalling the past. When he was growing up in south Vancouver, he was often a rascal at school and was sent to the back of the class for his mischief. He noticed that he was often accompanied at the back of the class by members of the Musqueam Nation, whose territory was close by. He recalls being impressed by his classmates, who knew more about subjects that were not taught in school—particularly about nature. He credits this experience to explain why he, a city kid, became interested in organic farming and following that, beekeeping.

The decision to shut down the cannery in 1979 was not taken lightly. The operation had occupied the back corner of the Burnaby warehouse where Ros, Roger and Natasha Villasenor worked away during the summer fruit seasons of 1977 and 1978, while we at the Brokerage Collective went about our food wholesaling business.

Gerry recalls that one of the things that made him stick with the co-op for so long was Roger's sense of playfulness. "Who else would invent pallet jack races?" Gerry said. "We bent the forks on the jack racing around the warehouse and were grounded for a while."

One of Roger's tricks was to build up so much steam from the cannery kettles during the day that the cloud would ooze down from the ceiling to reach floor level and settle there. "It's almost to the floor," he would yell, to let everyone know his game was successful. Pranks and diversions aside, the cannery workers still accomplished much production, and their goods were sold throughout the province.

However, there were sound business reasons for its eventual closure. "We needed to charge more, up to six or seven dollars a jar," Ros said. "That was more than the current non-affluent market would bear. Also we needed more staff at higher salaries."

By the summer of 1979 it had become apparent that the cannery could never break even in its present form. The co-op could invest more money into it to make a larger, more efficient and mechanized operation, or subsidize the present cannery from the other industries, or withdraw from the business entirely.

There were personal reasons for closure, too. "Those of us still working were getting tired of it," Ros said. "I don't think I fought very hard to keep it." To add weight to her decision, she had taken a wrong step in the warehouse one day and broken her foot while stepping off a wooden pallet.

"What am I going to do now?" she wailed to Gerry. She couldn't stand on the leg until she recovered.

"Why not work with me doing bookkeeping?" he replied. She agreed. They soon became the full-time bookkeepers to the industries.

Though I was not at the meeting in which the cannery closure decision was made, it was reported that Roger reacted strongly, stomping out of the room and yelling his curses into the warehouse. The others knew enough to wait until he had calmed down. They understood what Roger was feeling—so many of us had invested so much time into making the cannery work. Now we had to let it go.

The name Brokerage Collective had been retired by 1978, after which time we referred to it as a food wholesaler, and CRS Wholesale Distributor became its official name. Business was booming by 1979, and we rode the crest surrounded by the rise of other co-operative organizations in Vancouver: Co-op Radio (CFRO), which began in 1973 and broadcast from a heritage building at Pigeon Park; Edge City Woodworking Co-operative on Hastings Street; Baseline Type and Graphics Co-op; and several co-op tree-planting operations that provided income to the youthful and strong. Marginal Market's grocery store on West Sixth invited members and non-members to shop, while Agora Co-op on Dunbar had grown in membership, and the CCEC Credit Union, though small, was increasing their services.

New housing co-operatives were being constructed. One of the earliest was DeCosmos Village Co-op in southeast Vancouver—its first members moved into it in 1972. Another early housing project was named after Nova Scotia's Alex Laidlaw, an internationally renowned co-operative movement leader who had written the definitive study of co-operative housing in Canada. This housing co-op initiative was started in 1978 with financial support from Canada Mortgage and Housing Corporation (CMHC), and the construction work began in the spring of 1980, with members helping to plan and design the thirty-six townhouses near Boundary Road.

Community Alternatives Housing Co-op was an example of rural-urban communal living on a farm in Abbotsford and in a dwelling in Kitsilano—home for about forty residents. When members moved into the urban structure on West Second Avenue, it was with a sense of achievement. After wrangling with CMHC over building design specifications (including a sit-in in CMHC offices), the residents were able to build the co-operative principles behind Community Alternatives into their living arrangements. The building was divided into "pods" with small bedrooms and larger communal lounge and kitchen areas designed to foster interaction among the members—definitely not suited for nuclear family living. Other needs were met with a laundry room, library, meeting room and carpentry/crafts room.

The earliest of the Vancouver housing co-ops had been incorporated in 1970 and was designated Waterfront Consumers' Co-op. On the principle that it was cheaper to own than to rent, this co-op offered cheap housing by living communally. The original incorporation papers were filed and signed by our CCEC credit union instigator, Michael Goldstein, and the *Georgia Straight* was listed as one of the first directors of the co-op. By 1974 Waterfront's member-residents had purchased two houses—one of them, Maya House, was in Kitsilano, and the other was in Strathcona—and in the following years they added other houses in various parts of the city. The co-op was sometimes referred to as a "scatter" co-op, not at any one location. A vintage five-bedroom house on Charles Street in east Vancouver was one of Waterfront's acquisitions, and I lived there communally starting in 1981. In the spirit of co-ops, all the communal houses met on a sporadic basis to haggle over issues and budget members' money.

All of this lively, flourishing activity in Vancouver meant that customers were becoming familiar with the idea of co-op principles, and they wanted to support and strengthen our food wholesaler and our bakery in order to demonstrate these values.

Wild West Organic Harvest Co-op originated on Galiano Island with a local character, Lony Rockafella, and his partner, Joanna Newmoon, who lived in a commune called Daystar, which promoted organically grown produce. Ron Pither remembers that he admired Lony's entrepreneurial spirit as he started what Ron termed the first organic produce wholesaler in Canada.

Wild West women (and man and cat): Back row: *(left to right)* Lori Rudland, Jane Kalmakoff, Abbe Nielsen, unknown, Darcy Hamilton, Jane Preus. Bottom row: Unknown, Ros Sherrard, Diana Smith. The cat was later adopted by another Wild West worker, Sylvie Beauregard.

"He is the best mobile marketer, bar none, I've ever seen," Ron told an oral history interviewer in 2005. Ron explained that Lony would build a store in his truck box and take it to market. If a farmer's market was not available, he would organize one. "There's this huge truck box," Ron said, "and it's a beautiful store with a fireplace, café, incredible stuffed animals, a huge panorama which is an ode to recycling...[and] 75 percent of the food is organic."

Occasionally in the late 1970s, Lony would phone the CRS warehouse and talk to Paul or me about ambitious schemes to wholesale some products together. We thought he was crazy and strived to get off the phone quickly. But we were wrong. Lony began Wild West in Vancouver when its workers "were just street waifs, selling muffins," as Ron puts it, and the co-op survived. After its first few years, Wild West became a stridently feminist collective and, according to Ron, they wouldn't even sell to Lony, the founder.

Wild West continued to grow, and they employed many of CRS's friends: Ellen Hamer, Ros Sherrard and Abbe Nielsen, who we knew from the East End Food Co-op, and Darcy Hamilton and Jane Preus, formerly of Fed Up Co-op.

In 1979 CRS members decided we had outgrown the East Second Street warehouse and it was time to move to an even larger, twelve-thousand-square-foot warehouse on Odlum Drive in Vancouver. This high-ceilinged building inspired Ron Hansen, the co-op's first official manager under the new restructuring, to think about growing the shelving up, stacking layers higher and using a new electric forklift to reach cases. We had become big.

(Opposite) Things are looking up. Once the food wholesaler moved to a warehouse on Odlum Drive, Vancouver, the goods were stacked vertically and required new equipment.

ORIGINS OF WILD WEST ORGANIC HARVEST

— by Joanna Newmoon

Lony and I were living at "Primal Point" in 1973 to 1975-ish, and we realized that after a very hard winter, with the Daystar commune of anywhere from ten to twenty-five people living on carrots, potatoes, and greens from the garden (mainly planted by Hans and Jordan), we had to find a way to make a living besides cleaning houses and working at the Galiano Inn (for women) or clearing land and burning brush (for men).

So we left our goats and community for Vancouver, found no work, and then headed to the Okanagan with a tank of gas and no money, to pick cherries in Cawston. We picked for a month—going on to apricots and pears, sleeping by and bathing in the Similkameen River. And then we met Michael and Maureen, who were running Okanagan fruit to Vancouver. Brilliant! We lived in our truck and loved to be on the road. We started selling cases of fruit to co-op houses in Vancouver, quickly graduating to health food stores.

By September, we had such good business going that we rented a warehouse in Surrey and joined a co-op residence (owned by Colin, who built and ran Banyan Books), also in Surrey.

Yes, that's when Wild West Organic Harvest was born! Our phone message had the sound of a clopping horse and Dale Evans and Roy Rogers singing, "Happy Trails to You." Ron and Ira were two of the main folks that worked with us. Sometimes I would do thirteen deliveries a day!

The following spring we moved to Richmond—to Bob Boese's sprout factory—which had a greenhouse, a barn, and a walk-in cooler—and we thrived. I don't remember what year we moved to the First and Clark warehouse in Vancouver. By that time I'd wrecked my back unloading semis from Community Produce, so after a brief time at First and Clark, I moved back to Galiano and stayed at Retreat Cove.

There are still guys in our lives that worked at Wild West and are still connected with us—Arthur Kelly and Mike O'Brien. They were also at First and Clark. Lony stayed a few more months and then he, too, moved home. So now what? Travelling markets, that's what! We teamed up with Sky and Akasha and had two three-ton trucks. We set up our depot in an old motel in Departure Bay. Each room had a function: there was the "banana ripening room" and the "dry goods" room, and the garage became the walk-in cooler. Each week we drove to either the west side of Vancouver Island (Ucluelet, Tofino, Port Alberni) or the east side (Port McNeil, Sointula, Alert Bay), selling fresh produce, cheeses and dry goods out of a "bucket stand" (a plywood sheet with holes for the buckets, maybe fifteen of them), with couples switching routes each week. Then Sky and Akasha had their first baby, Surya, and Grandma (Lola Haenen) joined their team. Then more babies started to arrive, so we set up a weekly market at the Community Hall on Galiano. This was around 1979, and we bought the land that Daystar is now on from Olie Garner, the first building to go up being the walk-in cooler—essential.

Daystar started out as a truck with the bucket racks and me in a snowsuit, selling one day a week. Lony would set up, then go look after kiddos. I would sell during the day, then go home and look after kiddos while he took down.

By the mid-eighties, we knew we could make a living on Galiano selling food, and voila, Daystar Market was built and born! Don Seed, John Levi, Myron and Jordan (to name a few, with much gratitude) were the main builders, and Mo Fraser, Val (still there!) and Gina Wilson (yay, she's back!) worked with me cashiering. Yes, there were many more involved, and I'm sorry my memory has faded—but not my joy and gratitude!

Chapter 14

TITO'S YUGOSLAVIA

I left CRS in the winter of 1978/79 to work at a secretarial job that I loathed in order to earn the money to visit Yugoslavia. Many of us had been long interested in this country, because it was a model for worker ownership of its industries, and we hoped to learn more by making contacts and visiting them.

As I recall, I was disenchanted with CRS Workers' Co-op at the time as a result of a December 15, 1978, annual general meeting that explored a divisive issue—the allocation of surplus. The surpluses in question were for the years 1977 ($17,337) and 1978 ($39,730). In a lengthy and unsigned financial report it appeared that the decision had already been made to allocate the 1977 surplus to management as a bonus. The 1978 surplus could be retained by the co-op or allocated as a bonus to the workers. Though the financial report recommended that the workers receive a bonus, the mood of the meeting swung toward retaining the surplus within the co-op.

The division of management and workers vying for the same pot of money was unsettling for me—it did not respect the spirit of kickbacks, the money we had taken from our salaries (when we had grant funding) and loaned to the business from us, the original workers. It became clear that we would never see those loans returned to the individuals who had made them. Granted, it had never been promised that we would see the money again, but nonetheless it was disappointing. The ultimate decision to retain surplus was for the good of the co-op, and it was likely the right decision in the long run, but I came away disgruntled, knowing that I would have to continue my secretarial job in order to generate necessary income.

It was ironic that I was taking my secretarial salary from a quasi-governmental business, the BC Assessment Authority, in order to enrich my education of worker-owned businesses. Moreover, the work that I was doing, typing and filing, was trivial. I questioned the usefulness of such an organization that appraised homes and buildings in a bureaucratic, laborious manner solely to provide municipal governments with a figure for property taxes. How was this performing socially responsible work? I asked myself.

My arrogance—whether justified or not—must have shown, because after five months there I was given two weeks' notice, and I stomped out, never to look back on such employment.

The clamour rose into the vaulted ceiling of the Trieste train station. Mob voices. A human din of yelling, crying and thumping of feet. The train was at rest and I sat alone in a compartment bound for the Croatian city of Zagreb in Yugoslavia. I peered out to the platform but could see no one, and I nervously clutched my Swiss army knife, which I had used to slice salami bought from a kiosk vendor at Milan station. The blade had already proved useful. A leering Italian man had sat opposite me on the way to Venice and, flashing his white teeth, had engaged me in conversation using limited English.

"When the train goes through the tunnel, I will kees you," he said, grinning. That's when I brought out my knife and used it to clean my fingernails.

"I will not kees you now because you have a knife," he announced, crestfallen.

I knew then that, if I had to, I could take care of myself on this trip.

The man left the train in Venice, calling out endearments and promising to write, even though I had not given him my address. I was due to meet Dana in Zagreb after the train crossed the Italian border much later on that night, and I knew he would laugh at the story.

We were calling this a study tour. Much of Yugoslavia's industry at that time, 1979, was owned by its workers, and it offered interesting models for worker self-management. We had made arrangements in advance to view some of the co-operatives and maybe meet with academics and leaders of industry to learn more.

Josip Broz Tito, the country's leader and the man who had guided Yugoslavia through World War II, was still in power. This country was an anomaly: a non-aligned socialist country that was neither Soviet bloc nor western capitalist. Yugoslavia danced on the edge of communism but never shut itself behind an iron curtain like the rest of eastern Europe. Tito's presence in the national fabric was as difficult to ignore as his name on the fifteen-foot illuminated sign that marked a hillside in the Croatian town of Split. The real strength of the country lay in the worker self-management system. Only a common and impartial system such as this could have united the six republics, two autonomous regions, numerous minorities, four national languages and three major religions into pursuing a mutual goal.

The roar of the mob increased. It was coming toward the train. Was it a riot? A civil war? Centuries-old feuds ran deep in Italy. Through the window in the train's corridor, I peered out and witnessed an extraordinary sight: men and women of all ages, carrying bundles, backpacks and suitcases, dressed in what appeared to be three or four layers of clothing on this warm spring evening, running clumsily up the platform, shouting and grunting with exertion. The swiftest of the runners had reached my compartment at the front of the train, and they surged aboard, displaying big grins.

I backed into the compartment and sat down. It was the right thing to do. Within seconds the wave of humanity had surrounded me, with people wedging their bundles under the seats, jamming their bags onto the overhead shelf, doffing at least one article of clothing and then sitting on it, all of this accompanied by jeers, sighs, grunts and rapid-fire conversation. The latecomers, finding no room in the compartments, hunkered down in the corridor. They were Yugoslavians heading home from Italy. It was my first encounter with them and it was bewildering.

One man, who appeared to be wearing two fedoras, one on top of the other, placed his giant suitcase squarely on the floor between the seats. Glaring at the two women on either side, he announced, "Cheka cheka." Even with my limited knowledge of Serbo-Croatian, I understood this useful phrase. It could mean anything from "Wait, wait, you idiot" to "Move over, ladies." Turning around, he insinuated his bottom into the remaining few inches of seat and rested his feet on the suitcase. He smiled at me and pulled out a bottle of *rakiya*, the powerful Yugoslavian brandy. This was passed around the compartment, and when it got to me, I took a swig.

Apparently this was the friendly gesture the group had been waiting for. A woman with gold hoop earrings asked me where I was from. "She's from Canada!" A ripple of nods moved around the crowd and then two of the passengers took up animated conversation, glancing my way at intervals. A curly-haired young man asked me in a language that mingled both English and German whether I would do them a favour. Could I put some of these, their wonderful items purchased in the western shopper's paradise of Trieste, into my luggage? At least until they had crossed the border? "Thank you so much."

The rakiya man offered me one of his fedoras and mimed how I was to place it casually next to my purse. A woman with dark circles around her eyes (too much nightlife in Trieste?) shoved her bag under my seat. Soon I was surrounded by unusual clothing in a variety of sizes, and on my lap I held a box bearing a toaster.

It was a relief to know that the unruly mob that had terrified me in the Trieste train station were simply cross-border shoppers who hoped to pass through Customs without paying fees or being punished for their capitalist activity. I speculated that most of them would sell these consumer goods in the public marketplaces of Beograd, Serbia, where fashion and toaster technology had not caught up to the west.

At the border, uniformed Customs officials merely glanced at my passport stamped with the official visa that had cost me great bureaucratic pains to acquire, but they asked searching questions of the other occupants. Obviously somebody had ratted, because one passenger was called out of our compartment into the crowded corridor to account for the contents of a rogue suitcase held together with string. Sweating profusely, the man kept up a rapid and lengthy explanation that appeared to be wearing down the officials. Eventually they departed, squeezing through the hordes.

As the train lumbered on into the Croatian countryside and night fell, the passengers hastily repacked their bags. The toaster was snatched back by its owner, the bottle was passed around again, and silence, broken only by snores, settled over the group.

I remained awake, fighting the effects of the brandy. No specific arrival time for Zagreb had been given since the train was often delayed at the border. Dana was to meet me around 2 a.m. at the Zagreb station, and if I missed my stop, I might end up in Serbia without the language or the transportation to get myself back to Croatia. I noticed uneasily that the many stations we stopped at in the dark had no signs to indicate their location, and there was no friendly conductor to call out the halts. Midnight passed, then 1 a.m. Surely we were getting closer.

I realized it was going to take me time and effort to extricate myself from the crowded compartment, so I decided to gather up my few things in advance: one backpack with a foam mattress tied on the outside and one purse containing notebook, toiletries and salami. My travellers' cheques and passport were tucked into a money belt at my waist. Stepping over the sleeping passengers, I watched my now-vacant seat be quickly enveloped by the others. I set my luggage by the exit door. The train chugged on—it was 2 a.m., then 3. The train pulled into yet another darkened station. I hesitated. It was nearly 3:30 a.m. Had I missed Zagreb? Not a sound could be heard and no one disembarked. I clicked open the door and prepared to climb down. Suddenly a man on a bicycle wheeled up to the train and braked hastily.

I had practised my sentence: "Ovai ye Zagreb?" I called out to him. "Is this Zagreb?"

He stared at me, then shook his head. "Nay," he replied. I was proud of myself. The language lessons had paid off.

In the corridor, snoring individuals were attempting to sleep standing up; it seemed to be a useful skill in this country. But adrenaline was keeping me upright. Finally the train chugged into another station. Though dimly lit, it looked larger than the preceding one, and a kiosk selling candy and mineral water was open to customers. I disembarked with a few other passengers and looked around. No Dana, but the conductor materialized at my side and told me that yes, I had reached Zagreb.

Dana had left home in Vancouver many months earlier for a much longer journey through Africa, and we had made this date before he left. We had followed up by writing fat, informative letters to one another. I envisioned myself alighting at a grand central station bathed in light to the sounds of a full orchestra while rushing into his welcoming arms.

So much for dreams. The kiosk lady, awakening from a doze, looked pleased to see me, especially since no other passengers were interested in her wares. The minutes ticked by, during which time I pondered the miracle of how two people could fly halfway around the world from different locations and expect to meet at a railway station in a faraway country. He was late, I told myself, and had fallen asleep. Not to worry.

In this unexpected quiet interlude I wandered to the station portal and gazed at the tiled roofs of a sleeping city. As I watched, a light came on in a window, then another. A shop—perhaps a bakery?—illuminated a back room, and I could see silhouettes moving within the glow.

When a lone taxi finally rumbled toward the station over the silent streets, I strained to see its passenger. I caught a glimpse of a man dressed in a lumberjack-style, plaid flannel shirt. Who else would wear such a garment in Yugoslavia but a touring Canadian?

I smiled.

While in Yugoslavia, who would wear a lumberjack-style, plaid flannel shirt? Only a Canadian.

At that time, 1979, the Yugoslavian people lived and worked under an economic system that allowed them social ownership of the means of production, the right to make collective work decisions through their own elected bodies and the right to determine allocation of their enterprise's income.

Decision making, Dana and I learned, began at the most basic level—in the kitchens of the large restaurants, on the factory floors or behind shop counters—by the people who worked there daily. All over the country, on storefronts, offices, hotels and trucks, we saw the acronym OOUR in front of the name of the business. The initials stood for *Osnova organizacija udruzenog rada*, or Basic Organization of Associated Labour. These OOURs or work units voluntarily combined to form the larger enterprise. As visitors, our arranged itinerary included a visit to the enterprise Soko-Nada Stark in Beograd, a firm that produced chocolates, biscuits and Turkish delight. Five OOURs in various parts of the country combined to contribute their labour and products to that enterprise. Each of the five was a separate integrated work unit with its own name, its own decision-making process and even its own soccer team, but the products were all marketed under the name Soko Stark.

Some of this was familiar to us in our roles with CRS—for example, the fact that most of the decisions made at Soko Stark affected the people's daily lives: things like job assignments and conditions, distribution of surplus, hiring and firing. Bigger policy decisions, such as planning, investment and research, began their circuit of discussion by the Workers' Council, an elected body of workers' delegates. The economist Branko Horvat had described this hourglass model in his signature paper "Workers' Management," and I was delighted and overawed at the prospect of meeting him while we stayed in Beograd.

Horvat explains the hourglass model in this way. If we imagine the basic work units at the top half of a sandglass, generating ideas like grains of sand, then we must imagine the Workers' Council as being at the nexus of the hourglass through which those grains are flowing. At the other end of the hourglass sits the hired management or executive board. On occasion the hourglass is turned over and management, the hired experts, will originate various plans and proposals that flow once more back to the Worker's Council for comments and clarification. Ideas may require referring to a committee, which may return its findings to the council once more.

Based on our own experiences with worker-managed co-operatives in Canada, we had visions of voters dropping with exhaustion as a proposal entered yet another revision and no consensus had yet been reached. It was all too familiar.

When we arrived in Beograd, the capital of the country and the major city in Serbia, we coughed up the funds for a posh hotel after previously camping in a leaky tent or staying at bed and breakfast places. Unfortunately, we were not able to enjoy our comforts. On the night of our arrival, Dana fell ill with stomach pains, and I rushed him to a nearby hospital, where the pains were later diagnosed as appendicitis. At the Second Surgical Unit, he was treated by a Serbian doctor who had studied in Texas and had a high opinion of his diagnostic abilities.

"I poke him here, like so," the doctor told me, demonstrating on Dana's exposed stomach. "'Oww,' he said to me...so I know right away. No other American doctor has examined him in this way."

The doctor's pride notwithstanding, the important thing was that Dana's operation was successful, and he remained in the crowded and noisy ward of the hospital for three more days. Dana recalled how he spent this hospital time:

> Of all the places we visited to learn about worker self-management, I got the most detailed information from being in the hospital. Wandering the halls during recovery, I came across a bulletin board. You'll remember that the system gave many responsibilities to enterprise councils that would have been handled by a central bureaucracy under the Soviet system. So this bulletin board had listed all the criteria they were going to use to allocate all the housing units that had been assigned to the hospital for its workforce: whether a person was currently in overcrowded or otherwise substandard housing, how far they currently had to travel to get to work, et cetera. At the time I actually knew enough Serbian to understand most of it. Anyway, you might call it a serendipitous appendectomy.

Dana Weber proudly reveals his appendicitis bandage after an unexpected stay at the Second Surgical Clinic in Beograd, Yugoslavia.

Our visit with Branko Horvat, the famous economist, had been scheduled for exactly the time that Dana was in hospital. He urged me to go ahead with the interview, and I found my way to the Institut economskih nauka (Institute of Economic Sciences) at the arranged time. Branko and I sat in comfortable armchairs, but I was nervous. I was out of my depth in discussing economics, and I feared he would resent the intrusion on his busy life. He talked; I listened. I asked a few questions; he answered. We communicated in a mixture of English and Serbo-Croatian, and because I was intimidated by his knowledge, I took no notes.

Later, when Dana asked me to recount my meeting, I couldn't remember a thing, much to his disgust. Fortunately, Branko had presented me with a copy of one of his signature papers, "Workers' Management," and Dana and I could read and discuss this at length, readying ourselves for the mini-presentation that we would give to the others when we returned home.

Chapter 15

WHAT HAPPENED THEN?

After my return from Yugoslavia in late 1979, a lethargy settled over me. Overall, the two months we spent there had been somewhat disappointing. The rich and complex history of the many factions that made up the country had been unsettling. It could be hindsight, but perhaps we sensed as we visited Croatia, Serbia, Bosnia and the region of Kosovo that the potential for civil war was brewing, sparked by the diverse religions and ancient feuds. The tours through the various worker-managed industries that were running the country had been insightful but had not encouraged us to return to CRS full of inspiration.

Both Dana and I had worked hard to earn the money to take this expedition in the very human belief that mightier works than ours were happening far away from home, and that we would be enlightened by travelling thousands of miles to view them at a new destination. Again in hindsight I realize that our most enlightening and inspiring work had already happened much closer to home in the process of building our own successful industries.

Now I was at a loss for a direction in life, though I wanted to break into the world of publications as a freelance writer, and it seemed that our recent experiences in Yugoslavia had opened a door. In 1980 Dana and I collaborated on an article titled "Yugoslavia Has Model for Poland's Solidarity" that was published in the *Vancouver Sun*. I also wrote a travel article about our journey from Croatia's touristed coast to Sarajevo, a crossroads of cultures, and this was published in *The Globe and Mail* travel section.

While these published works were satisfying, I couldn't live on their proceeds, and as my co-workers at CRS were still my friends, I turned to them for employment. I worked temporarily in the food wholesaler's warehouse with Marty Frost, who had just started, and with Ron

Hansen, Gordon Truscott, Fred Weihs and Dilys Bowman. I also worked part-time on retail for the morning shift at Uprising Breads Bakery. I continued as a member and volunteer at the East End Food Co-op that was thriving on Commercial Drive.

Marty Frost joined the co-op in 1979, and his management skills were put to use in the Odlum Drive warehouse office. When Marty began his employment, CRS upheld the principle that each worker should have experience in other aspects of the co-op. According to this plan, he began by spending a few days with the bookkeeping collective of Ros and Gerry before transferring to the bakery. His first experience was on night shift with Nestor who, in Marty's words, "flipped" when he looked at the bread order that the day-shift workers had posted on the board and he realized that he and Marty, a totally untrained new worker, were the only staff assigned to produce 1,050 loaves that night. While Nestor raged at the idiocy and lack of planning, Marty began weighing ingredients, preparing them for use in bread making. After Nestor calmed down, he apologized and acknowledged that the pre-weighing of ingredients was a new and good idea. They finished all the baking by 1:30 a.m., Marty recalls proudly, and he continued to work at the bakery, enjoying the experience. Three months later Ros and Gerry put out an enquiry: Where's Marty? He was supposed to work with us!

While we had grant funding, we could do and learn out of our comfort zone, and we were allowed to make mistakes until we got it right. With the economic downturn in the early 1980s, much of the heady, innovative project grant funding had dried up. Some grants survived, though, in the form of incentives to employ students in the summer months, and a bastardized version of funding, the so-called "top up" grants for non-profit organizations.

Gerry Dragomir had moved from CRS Workers' Co-op to CCEC Credit Union in the role of loans manager, so he was in a good position to view the financial confusion of the times. In an interview in 2016, he said, "People changed [in the early 1980s]. The generation that followed ours went to business school. We got old."

We were now in our thirties, and there was a move by many of our age to seek comfort, to settle into a permanent home or a housing

What Happened Then? — 143

The CRS Workers' Co-op food wholesaling warehouse on Odlum Drive in Vancouver. Moznik Trucking was one of our favourite carriers.

co-op or move to the country where land was still cheap. In the various co-operative organizations, including CRS, some talented founders moved on to other jobs, leaving the wholesaler and the bakery in the hands of newer, though no less enthusiastic, workers.

Gerry's speculation was that the co-op had stopped being dynamic—that as founding workers we had all experienced the same pains in order to grow the industries, and we had strived to remain equal. We had each tested new ideas by working at the various jobs, and we had either found the ideas wanting or applied them to our work. When new members joined the group, they would look at the existing work practices and ask themselves, "How can we do this better or faster or cheaper?" These efforts at change were sometimes dismissed by long-term members with a brief, "Oh, we tried that years ago and it doesn't work."

Early co-op members were experiencing burnout from long hours at low pay. Some had thought the work would be more politically vigorous and were not ready for the drudgery of stacking cases in the warehouse or filling the night shift's bread orders. A few withdrew from the co-op to move on to related organizations. Two workers who stayed were to have a big impact on the co-op: Gordon Truscott worked in the warehouse, while Maureen Collier worked at the bakery and then took on a role with the bookkeeping collective. In the 1980s Gordon became manager of the wholesaler, while Maureen became its financial administrator.

Although the original social goals were static, the business side of the equation was expanding greatly. The CRS food wholesaler moved to an even bigger warehouse, carrying even more goods and becoming one of the province's largest wholesalers under the name of Horizon Distributors.

In 1982 delegates from all over Canada gathered in Ottawa for the Co-operative Future Directions Congress, a three-day meeting that was the culmination of a four-year planning task force involving several major organizations. We had been alerted to it by Keith Jardine, who was doing co-op and credit union development work.

Several members of Vancouver's new wave of co-ops attended. Dana and I represented CRS, though neither of us was actually working with CRS at the time. He was helping to set up a food co-op in a low-income housing development in Burnaby, while I was on the board of directors of the East End Food Co-op and was about to take on a grant-funded job in administration at Co-op Radio. Sheila McDonnell, the East End's store manager, also attended the congress, as did Abbe Nielsen, who had worked with Wild West Organic Harvest Co-op and was now studying at Simon Fraser University.

With the exception of Keith, all the conference organizers were older than we were—in their fifties or sixties—and the majority of the participants were also mature and represented the old guard: Federated, Wheat Pool, and Oshawa Autoworkers. Apparently we youngsters were the hope for the future, and sometimes at the conference I felt as if I had "new wave co-ops" written in neon on my brow.

We were to study a draft vision for the co-op movement while meeting in small groups, then report back to the other 350 delegates. I was one of three women in my small group—three out of twenty-three

WHAT HAPPENED THEN? — 145

After working at Uprising Breads Bakery for eighteen months, Gordon Truscott moved on to warehouse work on Odlum Drive in 1980, following Fred Weihs' departure to manage a co-op on Baffin Island. Gordon became business manager through two warehouse expansion moves, finally resigning in 1993. He humbly takes credit for inventing the new name of the wholesaler, Horizon Distributors.

in total. As I looked at the circle of suits and ties around me, I had serious doubts. What views could I hold in common with a pipe-smoking gentleman from the Wheat Pool, Co-op Union of Canada vice-president Ray Siemens, and an elderly representative from a prairie credit union? This group assumed that my proclivity was toward smaller, more socially oriented co-ops, and this sparked many a discussion, notably around the issue of a co-op becoming a viable business presence before it could become a tool for social change. That particular debate continued at an Ottawa restaurant in which several new-wave co-operators shared a meal and drinks with an older co-op and union organizer. He provoked an invigorating discussion and then departed the table early, leaving us to pay his bill.

ISADORA'S CO-OP RESTAURANT ON GRANVILLE ISLAND

Though Isadora's Co-operative Restaurant did not open its doors until 1982, the basic ingredients of the venture had started much earlier by some members of Community Alternatives, a housing co-op in Kitsilano, who sought to start a restaurant that every diner could own. The Granville Island Trust wanted more facilities for families in the newly reconstructed public area of the island. The Trust approached Theodora's Restaurant, a busy sandwich and supper place at Burrard and Fourth, which was operated by Total Education, an alternative high school. Theodora's agreed to partner and form a family restaurant serving good homestyle cooking. For a one-hundred-dollar share, diners could buy into the restaurant and receive twenty-five dollars' worth of free meals a year. The regular menu was affordable, but because of Vancouver's competitive restaurant market, Isadora's was forced to close in the 1990s.

However, a wildly popular dish that had originated with Isadora's chefs survived to carry on the name—their Go-Nuts burgers, made of walnuts and vegetables, can still be found in the freezer section of some grocery stores.

The next day the small groups were asked to analyze at least one of sixteen priorities that ranged from social and economic responsibilities to how to get co-op curriculum in the schools, and we were assigned topics in a seemingly random order that lacked common sense. Our East End Food Co-op manager, Sheila, flounced out of her small group grumbling about how twenty-seven presidents and CEOs of major co-op organizations had been gathered to discuss the role of emerging co-ops.

"What are they going to know about it?" she asked. But then she grinned. "Maybe we should ask them to set aside one percent of their surplus to support emerging co-ops…" and she went off humming.

It was estimated that the average congress participant had between fifteen and twenty-five years of experience in co-ops. Given the extent of the history in the room, I finally realized that some of these men had grappled in years past with the same principles and questions that faced us that day. It was humbling to find that very often we were all on the same side.

For such a pivotal event as a major national congress, the results were not startling. However, the vision that we were to take back to our co-ops made some of the same key points we had worked with for years: power rooted in the communities, equality and respect for one another.

In 1984, when I started work as a writer in the publications department of BC Central Credit Union, I considered it to be a natural extension of working with the co-op movement—in this case a financial co-operative—despite its corporate hierarchy. I found that Keith Jardine, formerly of the Fed Up Paid Collective, was also employed by the credit union central as a kind of "ideas guy."

Indisputably the experience of developing a workers' co-op spawned successful careers for many of its members. Our experiences had produced a profound and lasting effect on our lives.

Chapter 16

GOING FASTER, LIKE A ROLLER COASTER

As I mentioned in the introduction to this book, in 1999 I was asked to contribute a one-thousand-word article on the subject of co-operatives for the *Encyclopedia of BC*. I was out of touch with CRS at that time, because I had moved to Gibsons on the Sunshine Coast of BC and was pursuing the interesting but impecunious life of a newspaper columnist.

In covering the rich history of the many food, housing and producer co-ops in BC, I could allocate only a few sentences to each one. As I wrote about the success of CRS Workers' Co-op—I knew they still ran a flourishing business—I felt proud of what we had wrought. I knew that the business was now worth much more than the early days, when we struggled to pay ourselves. Pleased with the way the *Encyclopedia* article was progressing, I phoned the CRS warehouse (now called Horizon Distributors), expecting to check a few facts for accuracy. To my surprise, the voice on the other end of the phone informed me that it was no longer a co-op. They had wound down over the past year and were now privately owned.

Shock, sadness and a little indignation washed over me. What had happened to the principle of co-operative ownership? Why had no one contacted me or any other of the original shareholders? Who had bought it and at what price?

No answers were forthcoming, not that year or in the years to follow. Perhaps we didn't ask the right questions of the right people. Most of us had moved on in our lives and we let it go. That is, until I came to write this book. It was like reading a murder mystery and finding the last page, the whodunit, to be missing. I began to ask questions.

The entry in the *BC Encyclopedia*, after some rejigging and help from editor Dan Francis, read, in part: "In order to provide co-operatively produced goods and to provide employment for themselves, a

Vancouver workers' co-op was founded and later became a model for others. Owned and operated by its employees, CRS Workers' Co-op, incorporated in 1976, was still going strong as CRS Holdings (no longer structured as a co-operative) in the year 2000."

What had happened to the workers' co-op that it had become CRS Holdings? Snatches of information were to be found from my interviews with Gerry Dragomir in 2016 and Marty Frost in 2017. The co-op was overextended, had borrowed too much money, the workers needed pay raises, some key people had left—all contributing factors.

Marty Frost had joined CRS in 1979, overlapping with my own part-time work in the warehouse, which was then on Odlum Drive in Vancouver. Though he left the co-op in 1984, he returned in 1986 following Ron Hansen's general manager stint. In Marty's words, it was a time of slow acceleration in some areas and decline in others.

Through the late 1980s, CRS (the wholesaling function titled Horizon Distributors) moved through a succession of warehouses, each larger than the previous one, until they landed in an eighty-thousand-square-foot building on Winston Street in Burnaby with increased cooler and

Marty Frost *(left)* joined CRS Workers' Co-op in 1979 and became a general manager, seen here at a CRS celebration with member Tom Hinkle

freezer capacity. Horizon also found its niche as a brand name. A colour combination emerged to define the business: red and yellow, with yellow stripes through a red bar, the recognizable colours that were painted on the CRS delivery truck. With the thought that the co-op might repackage liquids such as corn oil and olive oil, a committee set about determining a brand name and came up with Red Canary, a throwback to the days of the cannery. The name and the project were not a success.

By 1994 revenue for the co-op was thirteen million dollars, but this financial picture was to roller-coaster for the next few years. A poor year that didn't realize projected sales was followed by a huge effort spearheaded by Horizon's manager, Gordon Truscott, to turn things around. The push succeeded, but the roller-coaster ride continued.

Nutrition bars were a hot item in the 1990s, and CRS decided to enter that market by manufacturing their own. Peak Bars were filled with nuts and fruit, using wholesome organic ingredients. But to venture into manufacturing a product required the purchase of equipment, set-up time and launch costs, as we had found so many years earlier with the set-up of the cannery. Profits dipped even though Horizon was still growing and sitting on inventory worth approximately one million dollars. The co-op needed money in the form of loans or investment, but under the terms of the Co-op Act at that time, outside investors were not allowed; you had to be working with the co-op to invest. Marty then came up with a way in which outside investors could place money in the co-op. Each unit—Horizon, Uprising Breads and Peak Bars—could have investors, allowing the co-op entity to own all three units but not take any direct investment.

Investment was necessary. "In the grocery business you have to be top dog," Maureen, the financial administrator, said in a 2017 interview. "You have to grow or you're driven out."

Peak Bars failed to provide the co-op with the desired diversification into manufacturing goods, and the co-op was hit by another whammy. Several key workers quit; salaries—or the lack of them—were the issue. Gordon, the general manager, also gave his notice. Morale was low and funds to repay investors were even lower. Maureen stayed with Horizon through these challenging times before going on sabbatical in

1996 and deciding not to return. The key personnel were replaced with new hires from outside the co-op movement who had the expertise to run the business, but did not always understand the principles behind the organizational culture. Maureen remembers that one new recruit who did grasp the bigger picture was Terri Newell, who was studying community economic development in the planning department of UBC before she was hired.

As a student, Terri had toured the CRS warehouse when it was on Vanness in Vancouver, and while there she applied for a job in accounts receivable. She quickly noticed that a study of the organization and its policies would make a good thesis topic. She was hooked and continued at CRS through its transitions, later becoming general manager.

When a Toronto businessman, Ron Francisco, offered to buy out the co-op, the staff was asked if they wanted to regroup and buy it themselves. Marty recalls that they did not. "Everyone was exhausted," he said. The vision was still there, Marty explained; the workers were still governing the workplace. They had adhered to a three-year planning process that had made the co-op bigger, but the promised increase in salaries for everyone was not forthcoming.

"We closed arrangements in November 1998 for the sale of CRS Holdings," Terri recalled. It was a difficult time. "We didn't sell the co-op for a grand profit and then divvy it up," she continued. "We had grown too fast to finance ourselves. The credit union was breathing on us." At that time there were fifty people on the payroll and they had each paid a two-thousand-dollar share to work there, money that was taken from their paycheques (a far cry from the 1970s original share purchase of one hundred dollars). When asked to increase their share purchase to four thousand dollars, plus take a ten percent pay cut, most opted out. Terri managed to retain a seat on the board after the purchase and continued as general manager. "I count it as an absolute effing victory that we salvaged it," she said. "It's the thing I'm most proud of. We could have lost everything."

Money from Francisco's purchase was paid out to the shareholders and to the recent investors, and a portion amounting to $125,000 was sent to CCEC Credit Union to support other co-operative projects. The Canadian Worker Co-op Federation, a national grassroots organization that supports the development of workers' co-ops, also received $75,000 of the money.

The Co-op Act was changed in 2000 to enable co-ops to sell multiple classes of shares, which would allow outsiders to invest in a co-op. Would this ability have changed the picture for CRS if it had been enacted earlier? Possibly. We'll never know.

Horizon Distributors, still based in Burnaby, sells across the country and has become a multi-million dollar business. The current warehouse sprawls over 150,000 square feet on Trapp Street where 127 staff members enjoy an attractive workplace that includes a lunchroom, a gym and a shuttle bus to the SkyTrain station. Ten of the staff (as of June 2018) are previous co-op members—some from the original 1999 sale, including Terri Newell, who continued as general manager without much interference from the new owner, and Anita Pollard, human resources manager, who Roger had hired in 1980 to work at the bakery. Seven of nine division managers are women.

Horizon offers six thousand items on wholesale, still giving priority to organic and natural foods as we had done in the past. Their next priority is to products grown or made in Canada, and following that, priority is given to those vendors who have marketing ability, since many unfamiliar products need promotional support. It's a reminder that good sales practices are essential, whether co-op or not.

"We adhere to co-op principles," Terri said. "The policies are mostly unchanged—respect for the employees, a good work environment... Our policies are our success."

Anita agreed. "The world has caught up with progressive policies," she said. "We have a decent workplace and so do other companies now." At Horizon it's up to the owner to look at the bottom line. "We don't chase dollars for the sake of it," Terri added. The system works.

In 2016 the company celebrated its fortieth anniversary with a reunion in Vancouver. Eighty-five people, workers from 1971 through 2016, turned out to hear stories about the old days and to schmooze with people with whom they had lost touch years ago. Just as in the old days, everyone chipped in to help. The reunion was organized by CRS founder Gail Cryer, long-time Horizon financial officer Maureen Collier, and Horizon human resources manager Anita Pollard. Paul Newman worked the sound equipment and ran the visual presentation put together by the organizers. A vast spread of food was supplied courtesy of Horizon and Uprising Breads.

Dana Weber spoke to the assembled audience about the early days, I read a few pages from this book about the cannery and the first steps of the wholesaler, and Marty Frost spoke about the later years. Horizon manager Terri Newell described the current business and how the current workers had not forgotten their co-operative roots. Elaine Young and Judy Harper from Fed Up (who had later worked at CRS) opened up the floor to other speakers. Gordon Truscott gave some entertaining memories; Carmen Rodriguez, sister to the late Nelson Rodriguez, talked poignantly about her brother's experience; while others told tales of late nights on bread shift at the bakery. The man who had purchased CRS, Ron Francisco, did not attend the reunion.

Also at the reunion was Katherine Ruffen from CCEC Credit Union, still going strong on Commercial Drive in Vancouver, though the man who had signed us up as CCEC charter members, Michael Goldstein, had passed away. Keith Jardine and Sue Colgate, originally Fed Up staff, were also there. On the table display was an acknowledgement of the hard-working and greatly missed members who had died: Roger Inman, Paul Phillips, Nelson Rodriguez, Ken Waldron and Benjamin Goldman were among those with whom I had worked.

The owner/general manager of Uprising Breads Bakery, Don McGinn, was also at the 2016 reunion. Ron Francisco had bought the whole package, food wholesaler and bakery, but as McGinn explained it on the day after the reunion, when he offered former CRS members a tour, Francisco wanted to offload the bakery, even though it was wholesaling products throughout the Lower Mainland. Don McGinn had been working at the bakery as retail coordinator since 1987, and he and bakery manager Dennis Mills met with Ron Francisco.

"Ron pushed a piece of paper with a price on it across the table to us," recalls Don, "and he said, 'Boys, I've got no interest in running a bakery.'" Don recalls that he took a deep breath, cobbled together the money and bought it. His first day of private ownership was August 1, 2000.

Uprising Breads is still at its original location on Venables, though in 1986 they mounted a complete renovation and annexed neighbouring storefronts to allow for more production area and more tables so that customers could enjoy the many sandwiches offered every day or drink the coffee that provides almost a quarter of the day's revenues. ("We hired a dedicated barista rather than go on with the drip coffee that we were selling.") Many of the original products first produced in the 1970s are still available: Christmas fruitcake that is wholesaled across the country, muffins, cinnamon buns and the best hot cross buns in BC. In 2005 the bakery annexed a plant a few blocks away in which the night shift makes twelve hundred loaves on a slow night and two thousand loaves on a Friday—for retail and wholesale.

When it was time for group photos at the reunion, I stepped up to pose along with others who had worked during the period of 1971 to 1979, those early exciting years that built the industries. Yes, we were all looking good, even if we were older and with more silver hair or bald pates than before. There is Will Mitchell in the front row, almost unrecognizable without his beard, kneeling alongside Dilys Bowman, with organic

CRS Workers' Co-op founders and members from 1971-1979 at their 2016 reunion party.

agriculturist Ron Pither next to them, wearing his T-shirt that boldly states "Farmed and Dangerous." His slogan reminds us that we all eat for a living. Paul Newman is at the end of the first row. In the second row a smiling Joan Makaroff and Debbie Eaton stand alongside Ron Hansen. Ros Breckner, Maureen Collier and Gail Cryer link arms in comradeship. In the back row are Gerry Dragomir, looking fit; Fred Weihs, who came from Ottawa especially for the reunion; Marty Frost, the co-op development guy; and then me, Jan DeGrass, peeping out next to Lee McFadyen, whose farm in Cawston had inspired us. Standing at the end of the row are Dana Weber, Gordon Truscott and Sheila Adams.

When the next group was called in front of the camera—those from the years 1980 to 1989—it was a revelation for me. In the photo lineup for the second time that day were Gail Cryer, Gordon Truscott, Maureen Collier, Will Mitchell, Dilys Bowman, Ros Breckner and Marty Frost, plus many others of my acquaintance who had been hired after I left the co-op. They are pictured along with bakery managers Isabelle Truscott, Joyce Chong and Dennis Mills. These were the people who had stuck with the co-operative to help it thrive and grow, just as we had planned so many years past. Silently, I thanked them.

CRS Workers' Co-op members from 1980-1989. Photo taken in 2016.
Front row: (*left to right*) Anne Brainerd, Carol Madsen, Ros Breckner, Maureen Collier, Gail Cryer, Gail Mountain, Alan Kelly. Middle row: Sage DeBelle, Will Mitchell, Dilys Bowman, Elaine Young, Janet Cooke, Anita Pollard, Rose Koyama, Joyce Chong, Sima. Back row: Dennis Mills, Isabelle Truscott, Heather McPherson, Don McGinn, Marty Frost, Jeanne Murphy, Tom Hinkle, Richard Vignola, Michael Brinsmead, Gordon Truscott.

Chapter 17

AND TODAY?

An apocryphal story made the rounds in the 1980s. In the early years of Fed Up, ideals ran high, and the warehouse was staffed by a women's collective of varying political persuasions. On one occasion a corporate credit directory representative phoned to make discreet enquiries as to Fed Up's financial health. After collecting the usual data—accountant's name, sales figures, type of business, et cetera—the interviewer hastened to ask question number 8C: Purpose of Business. After thinking for a moment, the Fed Up staffer confidently replied, "To overthrow capitalism."

Clearly the so-called "new wave" of co-ops from the 1970s has not succeeded in trouncing the economic structure of the West, yet here we are decades later—living in housing co-ops, depositing money in credit unions and shopping in co-op stores. We have also had the chance to congratulate many co-operative ventures on their fortieth anniversaries.

Many of the existing co-operatives that were started in the 1970s were primarily for housing. According to the Co-operative Housing Federation of BC (CHF BC), there are 260 non-profit housing co-ops in the province, mostly in Vancouver (2018 figures). Those smart buyers who moved into the mere handful of Vancouver housing co-ops years ago are now breathing a huge sigh of relief, because they live in affordable shelter in Vancouver's inflated housing market. Many of the former CRS workers interviewed for this book live in Vancouver housing co-ops.

Judy Harper, formerly of Fed Up and CRS, attracted my attention at the 2016 reunion in order to tell me that the Waterfront Consumers' Co-op was still doing well. It is one of Vancouver's oldest housing co-ops and owns several houses in various parts of the city, including my former home on Charles Street at Victoria Drive in the East End.

British Columbia has a healthy credit union presence, and these organizations consistently state in their marketing pronouncements that they are locally owned and controlled by their membership. CCEC Credit Union, which had its incorporation papers signed in the living room of the house on Pandora Street so many years ago, is still in existence on Commercial Drive. Long-time CCEC manager Jill Kelly wrote in the credit union's newsletter on their fortieth anniversary that when it was given its licence by Dick Monrufet, the Superintendent of Credit Unions, no one from that office or from the Credit Union Reserve Board or from BC Central Credit Union thought that they stood a chance. Who would put money into a credit union with such bizarre ideas as to offer no interest on investment? Even though proponents explained that they would offer below-market lending rates for co-operative ventures, no one in credit union authority thought this a viable model. CCEC Credit Union has since gone through some ups and downs, but it clearly demonstrates the need for such an organization, as it is still in existence while other credit unions have merged or folded over the years.

Here's a telling anecdote from Gail Cryer. She volunteered to sit on CCEC's credit committee and was nervous about the hiring interview, even though she had much experience with credit unions. But when the interviewers learned that Gail had been a founding member of the credit union, their attitude became increasingly respectful and they welcomed her aboard.

"It's not so much one up for me," said Gail. "It's one up for the credit union that's kept its charter members all these years."

The biggest change in this century has been in the area of consumer co-ops though the changes are not obvious. Mountain Equipment Co-op continues to sell outdoor recreation goods to its five million members as they have done since 1971. On a quiet section of Commercial Drive, a small tool-exchange library, a co-op in principle, shares useful utensils. Co-op Radio is still broadcasting and can be heard over the Internet. It is the food stores that have changed dramatically. The small co-ops or buying clubs of yesterday have evolved from their former pre-order, member-run roots—or they have met their demise. As an example, the Roberts Creek Resources Co-op on the Sunshine Coast was formed in the early 1980s and was run by volunteers who gathered to receive food orders from CRS Workers' Co-op and Wild West Produce. Members socialized at the community hall while they repackaged their grains from bulk sacks or slapped sticky peanut butter from pails into jars. The co-op continued on with volunteer help into the mid-1990s before closing, and it is still remembered fondly by former members.

So why did it—and many others—close? There are several reasons for this, primarily the burnout of volunteers doing the same unpaid labour over the years. However, here's another theory. We were the initiators of successful food wholesalers such as Fed Up and CRS that propelled organic, whole foods into the mainstream. I believe this development changed the very nature of the food industry in BC by making many more healthy products available. When Paul and I set up the CRS food wholesaler (now Horizon Distributors) many years ago, the only place a customer could buy, for example, organic tofu or alfalfa seeds for sprouting—or plain yogurt with no added sugar, or myriad other bulk foods—was at a specialty or health food store. That is, unless you were a member of a food co-op. Horizon, which distributes to many businesses as well as co-ops, was obviously on to a good product line, as they passed their first million-dollar sales mark by mid-1980s.

These days every supermarket stocks organic produce, juice and cheese, dozens of varieties of yogurt, and bulk bins for scooping seeds, nuts and grains. Customers had become more knowledgeable about the quality of what they were eating. They wanted to eat locally grown food or at least Canadian-grown food. They wanted whole foods, healthy foods, forcing the stores to stock what the market wanted. Once a shopper had tasted Tunnel Canary pears in their own juice, they knew fruit could taste better without added sugar. Once they had a taste of sourdough pumpernickel at Uprising Breads Bakery, they knew that bread could be hearty and nutritious. We created that demand, and in so doing, we created change.

Co-ops that order from Horizon still function in BC on Cortes and Hornby Islands, and in Slocan Park, Lumby and Bella Coola. The Sointula Co-operative Store on Malcolm Island that exists today was founded in 1909 by socialist Finnish settlers. In the Yukon, the Whitehorse Potluck Food Co-op is owned by the members. My former co-op, the East End Food Co-op, is weathering the competition and operates from a store on Commercial Drive. The Kootenay Co-op in Nelson celebrated its fortieth anniversary in 2015. (Read remarks from a Kootenay Co-op member in Appendix I.)

The "new wave" of co-ops did not bear out their initial promise of transforming society. Despite the existence of co-ops in every aspect of our lives, it is difficult for anyone to go through a day without a commercial transaction in a private enterprise. Usually the co-op circus practises a different balancing act. The acrobatics consist of keeping one foot firmly rooted in traditional commerce and one eye on a more humane vision. It is the co-op values that have survived and continue to inspire.

"Co-ops for me," said Gail in a 2018 interview, "were a lot about people learning to take control of their lives." By championing organically grown food, we were not only concerned with our own health and the health of the planet, but we were also taking a strong role in food

"All Shoppers Welcome," says the sign in the window of today's East End Food Co-op, operating on Commercial Drive.

Uprising Breads Bakery has occupied the corner of Venables and Commercial since 1976. The aromas of fresh bread and rich coffee provide the siren call to visit this neighbourhood landmark.

distribution that we hoped would support the farmers and bring food to the people. These co-operative values live on.

In a 1981 article for *Kinesis*, the newspaper of the Vancouver Status of Women, titled "Co-ops: Tool for Social Change?" I asked the reader: "Why support co-ops? What advantage is there in supporting a movement that resists capitalism with all the fortitude of a marshmallow?" I went on to say: "Their strength is in their survival, in what they can teach us, and in their ability to grow."

Growth is continuing into new areas and new ideas. Investing locally is the goal of the new community investment co-ops, a rapidly developing co-op sector.

Ever had that feeling of déjà vu? In talking with Mark Cameron of the Coast Car Co-op on BC's Sunshine Coast in 2018, I have a profound sense that the troubling issues and passion-fuelled goals of our early co-ops have continued to flame into this century. The Sunshine Coast's car-sharing organization is successful in providing a much-needed service in the use of co-op-owned vehicles. Sharing a car costs less, makes it easy to access a variety of vehicles, and saves on parking and maintenance

Where Jane Austen rubs shoulders with Karl Marx. The People's Co-op Bookstore on Commercial Drive has been in business since 1945.

costs. And, just as in previous decades, there's an attraction to members in that they have a say in the co-op's operation through democratically run meetings. But also, as in the past, the organization is always searching for more volunteers, they spend time fundraising, and they struggle with the logistics of being a non-profit organization under the Co-op Act.

"One thing that helps us," said Mark, "is the strong community support." Again, these are familiar words.

Car sharing is not a new concept in BC as Modo, a larger BC-wide co-op that was started in 1997, has shown great popularity. Their innovative idea of car sharing started out like many other co-ops, and they explain on their website how they found guidance in setting up their model. They turned to the seven co-operative principles (see page 118) that were originally developed by the Rochdale pioneers in 1844.

These guiding principles ring just as true today as they did back then. Welcome to the twenty-first century, co-ops!

May we each continue, in our own small way(s), to attempt to make the world a better place. —Gail Cryer, 2016

Photos

Wasn't that a party! The Uprising Breads Bakery Christmas party in 1977 was memorable as we were celebrating being in business for one entire year. Warehouse workers Paul Newman on bass and Fred Weihs on button accordion provided the music.

PHOTOS — 163

Jan DeGrass (*left*) in her party clothes watching Dana Weber attempt to pop the cork on the champagne at the Uprising Breads Bakery Christmas celebration in 1977.

Janet Cooke (*left*) surprised Rose Koyama and Joan Makaroff on their last day of bakery work by tagging a little East End-style graffiti in their honour.

Ron Pither constructs bee boxes at Queenright Beekeepers workshop on East Hastings, Vancouver.

"It's a magical relationship with insects," says Ron Pither while applying a smoker to the bee hives up north.

The East End Food Co-op had its first home on Victoria Drive. Though small in size, it became members' one-stop shop for groceries, including Christmas trees.

There was a lot to learn for the volunteers stepping up for their shift at the East End Food Co-op. That's John Sawyer, one of the store's first co-ordinators, behind the counter.

The peeled, halved and cored pears were topped up with water before the lids were tightened, and then they were placed in hot, steamy canners. The stainless steel steam-jacketed kettle on the left was used for jam-making.

The racks of packed fruit jars were bathed in steam during processing then cooled by water spray to seal them.

Tunnel Canary's resulting fruit packed in water or honey was worth the effort.

We managed to prepare many fine dishes in the vintage kitchen of our communal house on Franklin Street. The sink had an original ceramic basin, the gas stove was difficult to light, the windows needed replacing and the coffee grinder on the counter was cranked by hand.

Bakery workers in or about 1986 or 1987. That's Isabelle Truscott and Robbie McGinn on the left and Hugh Wilkinson on the right. Beside Hugh is a woman called Nikki but her last name is lost to our aging memories. The person in the centre is also unidentified.

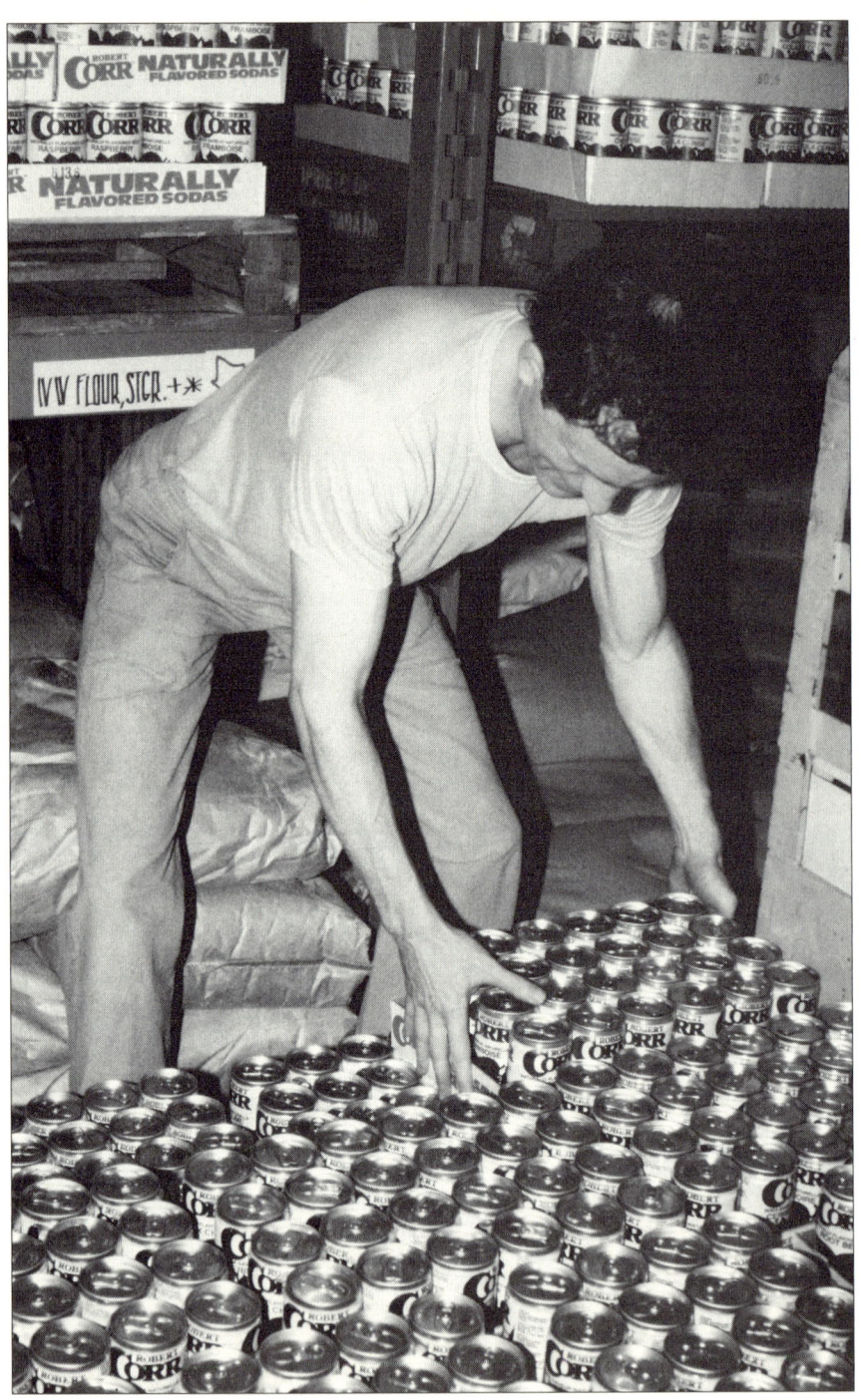
Cornered by cans: Dave Scott gets down to some serious warehouse work.

PHOTOS — 171

The East End neighbourhood welcomed Uprising Breads. Regular customers stopped by daily for coffee and pastries or grabbed a sandwich on their lunch break.

A hard day at the CRS office for warehouse worker Anita Pollard. She discovered that Post-it notes had no nutritional value and would not be considered for sale by the co-op.

Bread is always better than bombs is the message in this combined bakery and wholesaler CRS group photo in 1987. The workers' co-op proudly holds up its banner to be used during the peace marches of the 1980s.

CRS warehouse and bakery workers in 1983. Front row (*left to right*): Benjamin Goldman, Floyd Norman, Anne Brainerd, Jill King, Ann Mackay, Maureen Collier, Nikki. Middle row: Ken Waldron, Robbie McGinn, Roger Inman, Debbie Eaton, Debbie Hollett, Hugh Wilkinson. Back row: Ron Hansen, Gordon Truscott, Gail Cryer, Janet Cooke, Dilys Bowman.

Appendix I

ALEX BERLAND

REMARKS AT THE KOOTENAY COUNTRY STORE
CO-OPERATIVE'S ANNIVERSARY

In 2015, co-operator Alex Berland was asked to speak at a fortieth anniversary celebration for the Kootenay Country Store Co-operative, which grew out of the Vallican-Winlaw Food Co-operative. His speech went as follows:

> Back then, in 1975, the Vietnam War was a recent memory. In Portugal revolution had tossed out the dictators. But in Chile the military, with support from the USA, toppled a democratic government. China opened up and we were learning how they institutionalized co-operatives as an alternative economic model. Environmentalists from the so-called Club of Rome published *The Limits to Growth*, preceding Al Gore by a quarter of a century.
>
> Here in Canada, the counterculture flourished. Pierre Trudeau's Liberal government, riding a strong economy, recognized the need to build social infrastructure as well as physical infrastructure. They funded community development programs like Opportunities for Youth and Local Initiatives, which paid for co-op developers.
>
> In 1972 BC had elected Dave Barrett's NDP government. The NDP passed a new law on average every three days while in power. Both the Agricultural Land Reserve and Insurance Corporation of BC are still functioning. Corporal punishment was banned in all schools. They even had a Ministry for Co-ops. And the co-ops flourished so that by 1973 there were

fifty pre-order co-ops in BC. They were neighbourhood collectives; the coming together helped us reduce isolation, especially in rural areas (and it was tied to the back-to-the-land movement).

Here are the local co-operatives that were functioning at that time:
Vallican-Winlaw Food Co-op
Burton Arrow Lakes Food Co-op
Goat Mountain Food Association in Roseberry
Rock Creek Co-op
Nelson and District Consumers Co-op
Kootenay Lake Farmers Institute in Kaslo
Lardeau Valley Co-op in Argenta

Foodie culture was on the move: we learned about nutrition, switching diets, learning how to cook, organizing distribution networks—that was always a family affair, with every raisin individually fondled by our toddlers.

This was an era of self-determination. Here in the Kootenays, our food co-ops were only one facet of the counterculture. We built homesteads and community halls; we organized daycares and schools; we created libraries, theatre groups and film societies; we developed cemeteries and water-user groups.

We wanted to build an inclusive new society, without hierarchy. We distrusted authority and even leadership. But we had a planet to save, and much to do. So we needed to use our scarce time fairly and effectively. Without any experience, we were developing a modern form of governance: learning how to organize ourselves through authentic democracy. We stripped away the formalities but kept the spirit of *Robert's Rules of Order*. As General Roberts himself said, "Where there is no law, but everyone does what is right in their own eyes, there is the least of real liberty." We layered on "constructive criticism" and danced the dialectic, changing our use of language, making a pastime of debate. Put another way: surviving that collective consciousness-raising prepared me for every inter-personal conflict I encountered later in life.

At that time CRS Workers' Co-operative in Vancouver formed Fed Up, a federation of food co-ops that operated a warehouse to serve BC's pre-order co-ops. I cannot name all the leaders of the co-op movement, but I do want to honour Dana Weber, Rosalind Breckner and Paul Phillips, who built the movement. They introduced me to the work of Saul Alinsky, American author of *Rules for Radicals* (one of Barack Obama's sources). Buckminster Fuller, another seventies guru, said, "I seem to be a verb." Dana, Paul and Ros knew the doctrine, but aimed for propaganda by deed.

On reading the newsletter of September 1975, the recipes made me laugh: white beans and beer; black beans and rum; kidney beans in red wine. As Bonnie Baker reminded me, the kidney beans always had one free rock in every one-pound bag.

That edition of the newsletter had a three-page report describing big business interests and the impact of import restrictions on cheese—remember, this was in the period of consumer boycotts of Kraft products following a bitter strike. Lots of discussion about strengthening women's role in the co-op movement. Class consciousness. Letters accusing other co-op members of hippie communalism and rampant anarchy, instead of throwing off the chains of capitalism.

So much for the rear-view mirror. Jaimie asked me to talk not just about honouring our roots but also celebrating our growth. What is the link between the past, the present and the future? Change—yes, of course, but that is trite. I would say that it is the way we have lived our values while growing up that we should celebrate. All co-operatives (all over the world) are based on a core set of common values:

1. Self-help

In the early years, each co-op sent two people twice a year to work in the Vancouver Fed Up warehouse. We spent a week couch-surfing, packing the old truck for its provincial rounds with goods for remote co-ops. Volunteers in this "work-week collective" worked alongside rotating coordinators and the "paid collective" of bookkeepers and people calling up wholesalers. Packing orders, making meals together, we shared news from all over BC.

Back home in Vallican, we learned how to organize ourselves, to clarify roles and responsibilities and how to manage projects. We learned bookkeeping, communication, conflict resolution, systems. Terrific experience and many of us used this co-op background at responsible jobs in other sectors. Self-help was so important. Like all youth, we had big dreams. There was not much interest from the grown-ups, and sometimes outright hostility. We took some big risks. And we often succeeded—not always, but here we are today at this meeting. We created something from nothing.

2. Self-responsibility

A central feature of the Fed Up movement was self-direction. Co-op developer Marty Frost has said: "Co-op is not a Utopia, and it's not 'business as usual.' Every co-op you join represents another aspect of your life over which you are taking personal/shared control. That will not be accomplished without a little extra work, a little extra attention to your life." Is it worth it? Most definitely. You are building a point of strength in your community that will act to your benefit and to that of your children and grandchildren.

3. Democracy, honesty and openness

Back in the day, we worked hard to create a voice for everyone. Even the Work Week Collective, the weekly volunteers, made decisions—some food-related, others about how to run the warehouse; bigger issues went to our Provincial Council of all the co-ops, which met in different parts of the province a few times each year. (More couch-surfing, more love affairs, more recipes for exotic bean dishes.) Democratic member control is still a principle of our co-op. That's what this AGM is about. Giving authentic voice to members is what makes our form of organization different.

4. Social responsibility and caring for others

Okay—up to this point, our principles are mostly about us, the members. Now it gets harder. This is where we put our money down for other people to benefit. Our Community Giving programs demonstrate our role as investors in the social, environmental and economic well-being of our community.

It also costs more to fulfill our promise that "as an employer we strive to enhance each person's work experience." That costs more for wages and benefits and training and work-life balance and worker participation in decisions. When people mention higher co-op prices, I tell them I am proud that we strive to create good jobs in our community and share our profits to build worthy community projects. (But I know we have to work very hard to be price-competitive as well.)

5. Equality, equity and solidarity

This last core principle is about concern for our global community. Protecting the environment benefits everyone. The Kootenay Country Store Co-op has opened up the market for organic foods and now for True Local products, creating an ideal environment for stimulating a whole segment of the economy. Now most other retailers are climbing on board. It costs more.

Fair trade also costs more. It's that simple. How much we can each afford is a matter of individual conscience. But it is important to me that I have information to make a choice. The co-op gives me that.

At the outset we aimed for our co-operative to be so much more than the end of the grocery supply chain. It's the ability of an organization like ours to be responsive to social needs in our global community that makes me so proud to be involved.

So what will our co-op look like in another forty years? Maybe more multigenerational, probably more multicultural, maybe more internationalist. Likely operating at an even greater scale. These are the directions the members will need to consider.

Hopefully the values I listed will endure. Always, though, getting the balance right among collective benefit, sustainability, transparency and member engagement will be devilishly difficult.

As Paul, Ros and Dana would say, "We don't want to change our grocers. We want to change our lives." Together we are strong, my friends. Remember the ABCs of success—ability, bluff and courage. We will not be overwhelmed. We shall prevail.

Appendix II

FED UP CO-OPS OPERATING IN BC—1976

As reported in Fed Up's *The Catalist* newspaper, the following co-ops were in operation in August of 1976:

Abbotsford: Valley Food
Alert Bay: Hae Mae Co-op
Argenta: Lardeau Valley
Armstrong: Grub Co-op
Bella Coola: Stillwater
Burnaby: Snake Hill Co-op
Burton: Arrow Lakes Co-op
Cherryville: Cherryville Food Co-op
Cortes Island: Cortes Island Food Co-op
Courtenay: Glacier Fed
Crescent Beach: New Moon Co-op
Dawson Creek: Rootseller Co-op
Denman Island: Disc Coop
Gabriola Island: Rainbow Co-op
Galiano Island: Good Life Co-op
Hazelton: Hazelton-Kispiox Valley Co-op
Hope: Hope Co-op
Kamloops: Grateful Fed
Kaslo: Kootenay Lake Co-op
Lasqueti Island: Lasqueti Co-op

Likely: Likely Co-op

Lillooet: Lillooet Co-op

Lumby: Lumby Co-op

McBride: Blackwater Producer's Co-op

Mayne Island: Mayne Island Market Co-op

Mission: Dewdney Trunk Road Co-op

Nanaimo: Copia Foods

Nelson: Nelson and District Co-op

Ootsa Lake: Ootsa Lake Co-op

Penticton: South Okanagan Buyer's Co-op

Powell River: Phoenix Foods

Prince George: High Waters Co-op

Princeton-Cawston: Similkameen Co-op

Quadra Island: Quadra Island Co-op

Qualicum/Errington: Arrowsmith Foods

Quesnel: Grassroots Co-op

Rock Creek: Rock Creek Co-op

Roseberry: Goat Mountain. Food Association

Saltspring Island: Saltspring Consumers Co-op; Saltspring Storefront Co-op

Shuswap Lake: Shuswap Lake Co-op

Smithers: Watsonquah

Sointula and Malcolm Island: Islander Co-op

Terrace: Northern Neighbours Co-op

Texada Island: Texada Island Co-op

Thurlow Island: Coast Environment Co-op

Vancouver: East End Storefront Co-op; Eat Me Co-op; Kitsilano Co-op; Golden Harvest Co-op

Vernon: Kalamalka Co-op
Victoria: Amor de Cosmos; Fernwood Store
Williams Lake: Big Country Co-op
Winlaw: Vallican Co-op

Production Co-ops (Members of Fed Up)

CRS Workers' Co-op, Vancouver
Giant's Head Machine Shop, Summerland
New Star Publishing, Vancouver
People's Share Granola, Victoria
Press Gang Print Shop, Vancouver
Urban Design Centre, Vancouver

Other Member-Run Co-ops

Agora, Vancouver
Community Consumers Co-op, Burnaby
Fed Up Co-op, Vancouver
Fireweed Co-op, Atlin
Hope and District Co-op, Hope
Marginal Market, Vancouver
Ray-Cam Co-op, Vancouver
Tasu Co-op, Moresby Island

The newspaper noted that a list of the many housing and land co-ops would be too long to include, but that the following organizations could provide more information:

Coalition of Intentional Co-operative Communities
Community Alternatives
United Housing Foundation

These fifty-four Fed Up member-run food co-ops and eight non-member co-ops were listed in August 1976. By April/May 1978 the picture had changed, according to *The Catalist*, to forty-nine Fed Up member co-ops, including two in the Yukon and two in Alberta, and nineteen non-member co-ops. It is possible that the rise in non-member co-ops meant that co-ops were ordering directly through our CRS food wholesaler, or they could have been ordering from other wholesalers such as Vancouver's Lifestream Natural Foods.

Bibliography

B.C. Alternative, subtitled "A surfacing of energies and groups in British Columbia," n.d., ca. 1974.

The Catalist, Fed Up Newsletter/Newspaper: January 1976, February/March 1976, August 1976, December 1976, May 1977, August 1977, November 1977, April/May 1978, June/July 1978, August/September 1978, January/February 1979, March 1979, October/November 1979.

Chase, Stuart. "The Story of Toad Lane." Nanaimo, BC, n.d.

Co-op: The Harbinger of Economic Democracy, (Ann Arbor, Michigan), (May/June 1979).

Co-op Principles. International Co-operative Alliance adopted September 23, 1995. Short form from Co-op Housing Federation Canada resource publication.

CRS Consolidation, Growth and Extension, Industries. A report to the Special Programs Branch of Manpower about the LEAP grant job creation project, n.d., ca. 1974.

CRS Workers' Co-op, minutes book. 1976–1978.

DeGrass, Jan. "A Modern Joan of Arc Meets Kindred Spirits." Enterprise, July/August 1982.

―――. "Co-ops: Tool for Social Change?" Kinesis, 1981.

―――. "Co-operatives." In Encyclopedia of British Columbia, edited by Daniel Francis, 146. Madeira Park: Harbour Publishing, 2000.

―――. "Have You Ever Dreamed of Owning a Restaurant?" 9 to 5 Magazine, January 1982.

―――. "It's Back to the Books for Co-opers." Enterprise, May/June 1981.

―――. "Influence Not Power: Women Working Co-operatively." Credit

Union Way, November 1988. Award-winning article written to further co-op literature for the Canadian Co-operative Association.

———. "More Than Just a Housing Co-op: Community Alternatives." *Enterprise,* May/June 1985.

DeGrass, Jan, and Dana Weber. "Yugoslavia Has Model for Poland's Solidarity." *Vancouver Sun,* 1979.

Horvat, Branko. "Workers' Management." Institut ekonomskih nauka, Beograd, 1977.

Hunnius, Gerry. *CRS: An Evaluation.* Toronto: York University, 1975.

The New Harbinger: A Journal of the Co-operative Movement, (Ann Arbor, Michigan) (Summer 1978).

Patterns and Trends of Canadian Co-operative Development. The Co-operative Future Directions Project. Co-operative College of Canada, 1982.

Staples, R.S. "Yes...We Can!" A History of Mid-Island Consumer Services Co-operative. Nanaimo, 1980.

Weaver, Sharon. *Oral History Project: Creating Space, Re-creating Place: Rural Communities and the Back to the Land Movement of the 1970s.* Oral history interview with Ron Pither. Mayne Island, 2005.

Weber, Dana. *CRS Workers' Co-operative and its Antecedents: A Case History, 1971–81.* Updated in 1985 by author(s) unknown. Prepared for the Coady Institute Consultation on Workers' Co-operatives, August 1982.

INDEX

1697 Venables, 106
1868 Franklin Street, 50
2141 Pandora Street, 50, **51**
304 East First Avenue, 16
4025 East Second Avenue, 71

A

Abraham, Fred, 111
Adams, Sheila, 63, 103, 155
Africafe, 98
Agora, 92–93, 125
Amor de Cosmos food co-op, 15–16, 18, 19, 181
Antigonish Movement, 119

B

Ball Corporation, 15, 21
Bartlett, Jon, and Rika Ruebsaat, 89
beans, 27, 65, 74–75, 77, 99
Beograd, 138–40
Berland, Alex, 173-78
Bowman, Dilys, 142, **154**
Boyd, Denny, 113
Breckner, Ros, 12–15, 18, **25**, 50, 103, 125, **155**
Britannia Centre, 82
Brokerage Collective, 15, 30, 42–43, 50, 52, 55, 76, 80–81, 96, 125
Burn!, 82

C

Cabbagetown Co-op, 34
Canada World Youth, 50, 95
Catalist, The, 16, 63, 179-82
Cawston, BC, 19, 22, 53, 130
CC Grains, 76, 85
CCEC Credit Union, 56–57, 151, 153, 157
cheese, 65–69, **70**, 72
Chile, 55, 84, 104–6
China, 45–46, 55
Chong, Joyce, **155**
Coady, Moses, 119, 122
Coast Car Co-op, 160–61
coffee, 55, 96–98
Collective Resource and Services Workers' Co-operative, 11, 102
Collier, Maureen, 113, 144, 153, **155**
Commercial Drive, 65, 82–83, 106, 153, 157, **161**
Community Alternatives Housing Co-op, 7, 126, 146
Community Business Training, 77
Community Produce, 76
Compton, Hume, 120
Conference of Southern Ontario Food Co-ops, 34

Consumer Resource Services, 11, 102
Cooke, Janet, **109**, **155**
Co-op Act, 103, 150, 152
Co-op College of Canada, 77
Co-operative Future Directions Congress, 144
Co-operative Housing Federation of BC, 156

D

De Cosmos Village Co-op, 86
DeGrass, Rick, 31
Diet for a Small Planet, 52, 88, 96
Dragomir, Gerry, 63, 69, 142, **155**

E

East End Food Co-op, 41, 61–62, 142, **159**, **165**
Eaton, Debbie, 112, **113**, **155**
Encyclopedia of BC, 9, 148

F

Fairview House, 35
Fed Up, 16–17, 19, 35-38, 42, 47–49, 63, 80–81, 112, 119, 156, 177–82
Fed Up Council of Representatives, 36, 47, 93–94
Federated Co-operatives, 16, 119
Fernandez, Nestor, 104, 112
Fernwood, 63
FLQ, 41

Food Labelling Guidelines, 53
Ford, Cam, 103, 112, 115
Francisco, Ron, 151, 153
Fraser Valley Milk Producers Association, 44, 119
Frost, Marty, 141–42, **149**, **155**, 176

G

Galiano, 127, 130–31
Glen, Rod, 120
Goldberg, Michael, 42
Goldstein, Michael, 56, 126
Granville Island Public Market, 7, 89, 146
Greenpeace, 86–87
Gulf and Fraser Fishermen's Credit Union, 57, 97

H

Habitat Forum, 88
Hamilton, Darcy, 47, **127**
Hansen, Ron, 104, 106, 110, **113**, 128, **155**
Harper, Judy, 153, 156
Holdings, CRS, 149, 151
Hollett, Debbie **109**
honey, 15, 27, 58, 71, 73–74, 78, **168**
Horizon Distributors, 42, 144, 148–49, 152
Horvat, Branko, 46, 138, 140
House Savers, 19
Hub Co-op, 119, **121**

I

incorporation, CRS, 102–3
Inman, Roger, 14, **25**, 103, **113**, 153
Isadora's Co-operative Restaurant, 146

J

Jardine, Keith, 47, 121, 144, 147, 153

K

Kelly, Jill, 157
Kennedy, Murray, 59, 65
Kinesis, 84, 160
Kitchener-Waterloo, 31, 34–35
Kootenay Co-op, 159, 177
Koyama, Rose, **155**, **163**
Kraft, 67, 175

L

Laflamme, Phil, 58, 115
Laidlaw, Alex, 126
Lappé, Frances Moore, 52, 88, 96
LEAP, 21, 29, 40, 103, 115
Legare, Wendy, 113
Lett, Robin, 53–54
Lindow, Jimmy, 58

M

Mackay, Ann, 112
Makara, **85**–86
Makaroff, Joan, **110**, 112, **155**, **163**

Mao Tse-tung, 45, 64
Marginal Market, 53, 125
Marxist, 33, 104
Maxwell, Barry, 113
McDonnell, Sheila, 144
McFadyen, Lee, 19, 53, **155**
McGinn, Don, 153, **155**
McGinnis, Dick, 28, **44**, 45
Mid-Island Consumer Services Co-operative (see Hub Co-op)
Mills, Dennis, 153, **155**
Mitchell, Will, 93, 112, 154
Morrisey, Lara, 76–77, 85

N

Nestlé, 96–97
Newell, Terri, 151–53
Newman, Paul, 42–43, **44**, 48, **52**, 90, 103, **155**, **162**
Newmoon, Joanna, 127, 130–31
New School for Democratic Management, 77
Nielsen, Abbe, **127**, 144
Norman, Floyd, 13–14
North Vancouver, 13, 19, **20**, 28

O

Odlum Drive, 128, 142, **143**
Oliver, Sandy, 113
OOUR, 138
Oshawa Co-op, 34
Osteneck, Gerda, 58, 103, 115

P

Paid Collective, 37, 47–48, 80
party, CRS, 80, 114, 154, **162**
People's Co-op Bookstore, 83, **161**
People's Share Collective, 55
Phillips, Paul, 17, 19, 63, 177
Pied Pumkin, Pied Pear, 6, 89
Pither, Ron, **45**, 58, **60**, 106, 115, 127, **164**
Pollard, Anita, 152–53, **155**, **171**
Poole, Al, 14
Powell River, 94–95
Press Gang, 84–85
Purchasing Commission, 43

Q

Queenright, 9, 15, 43, 58–**59**, **60**, 103, 115, **164**
Quiroz, Carmengloria, 106, 112

R

Rationale, Grant, 50–51
Reunion, CRS, 152–55
Roberts Creek Resources Co-op, 158
Robert's Rules of Order, 37, 123, 174
Rochdale Principles, 46, 116–18
Rockafella, Lony, 127–28
Rodriguez, Nelson, 105, 153
Ruffen, Katherine, 57, 153

S

Scott, Rick, 6–8, 89
Seattle Workers' Brigade, 38, 76
St. Francis Xavier, 119
Sunshine Coast, 148, 158, 160

T

Tanzania, 53, 96
Taylor, Norman, 32
Toledo, Rosacruz, 106, 113
Truscott, Gordon, 144–**45**, 150, 155
Truscott, Isabelle, **113**, 155, **169**
Tunnel Canary, 7, 20, **25**, 29, **168**

U

University of Waterloo, 11, 31, 34
Uprising Breads, 9, 103, 106–**8**, **109, 110, 113,** 153–54, **160, 162**

V

Vancouver Co-operative Radio, **87**
Vancouver Folk Festival, 89
Victoria Drive, **61, 165**
Villasenor, Natasha, 106, 124

W

Waldron, Ken, 113, 153
Wallace, Keith, 65, **66**
War Measures Act, 41, 56
Waterfront Consumer's Co-operative, 86, 126–27, 156

Waterloo Food Co-op, 32, 36, 39
Weber, Dana, 15, 18–19, 40–42, **44**, 47, 50, 54, 103–4, 122, 139, **140**, **163**, 175
Weihs, Fred, 79–80, 123, 155, **162**
Weis, Liz, 101
Wheat Pool, 28, 44, 117–18
Wild West Organic Harvest, **127**–28, 130
Williams, Anne, **45**, 58, **60**, 115
Woodland Street, 63, 102

Y

Young, Elaine, 153, **155**
Yugoslavia, 132–35, 138, 141

Acknowledgements

This book owes a huge debt of thanks to the advice and encouragement of author, editor and mentor Betty Keller. I have attended her writing groups off and on since 1995 and two books have emerged. The first was my novel, *Jazz with Ella*, and now *The Co-op Revolution*—both helped along by critique from Betty and the other insightful writers who shared our time in the groups: Cynthia Sguazzin, Irene Harrison, Susan Garnham, Louise McKelvie, Judy Gitlin, Jo Hammond, Judith Hammill and Natasha Rosewood, to name a few.

Many thanks go to all the CRS Workers' Co-op members who I interviewed: Ros Breckner, Maureen Collier, Gail Cryer, Gerry Dragomir, Marty Frost, Terri Newell, Paul Newman, Ron Pither, Anita Pollard, Dana Weber and Fred Weihs.

And thanks to the many other former CRS members and friends of co-ops who contributed in some way: Alex Berland, Mark Cameron, Joyce Chong, Judy Harper, Jill Kelly, Joan Makaroff, Don McGinn, Gayle Neilson, Joanna Newmoon, Abbe Nielsen, Gordon Truscott, Keith Wallace and my enthusiastic foreword author, Rick Scott.

I also thank the many people who believed in the book: Caitlin Press publishers and Vici Johnstone's team, including my delightfully inquisitive final editor Christine Savage. Much gratitude goes to my dear friends Marlene Holt, Susan Pottery and Michele Wollstonecroft, who always take an interest in my writing, and Will Cummer who surprised me by actually reading the manuscript and liking it. Rolf Maurer was most encouraging from the beginning and sent me the nicest publisher's rejection letter I have ever received. Thanks go to William Gelbart for his insight into the nature of memoir and for directing me to the inspiration of Stefan Zweig's book, *The World of Yesterday*.

Most of the photos in this book were taken over a period of many years by many photographers. Unfortunately our collective memories don't provide details as to who took what and when. I provide my best guess here and give my apologies for any inaccuracies to these chroniclers of CRS activities.

Thanks to Floyd Norman for many of the early cannery pictures and he may have taken Queenright photos as well. My friend Beverly Pearl and my Aunt Florence Barlow also took some cannery photos. Later photos were taken by Gerry Dragomir, Gerda Osteneck and Brad Hyde. Dana Weber took photos while in Yugoslavia. Ian MacKenzie took photos of the bakery renovation. I took a few early photos using an ancient Agfa camera that let in too much light and some recent photos using my trusty Canon. At the CRS Workers' Co-op reunion in 2016 Jim Lemaistre was the official photographer and many thanks go to him for doing such a great job.

I dedicate this book to my parents, Al and Bette Naylor, though they have both long since passed away. My relationship with my parents was testy during the period described in the book. They disapproved of me working for such a counterculture organization when I could have become a doctor or a lawyer, in which case I could throw away the jeans and earn a decent salary. But when times were tough they always supported me with money, help or love. I couldn't ask for more.

Jan DeGrass
Sechelt, 2018

About the Author

PHOTO: KEN STRAITON

PHOTO: JUSTIN SAMSON

JAN DEGRASS writes in Sechelt, BC, where she is the former Arts & Entertainment columnist for the *Coast Reporter* and the current editor of *Coast Life* magazine. For the past twenty-five years she has written in every genre, from sparkling arts news to exotic travel narrative to a cookbook of potluck recipes. She received a national award for a business article that furthered Canadian co-operative literature, and she was a winner for Best Coverage of the Arts by the Canadian Community Newspapers Association. She is the author of a credit union history book and her first novel, *Jazz with Ella* (2012), based on her student experiences in Russia. Her short stories have appeared in *Canadian Living*, *Chatelaine* and *Room*.